BOBBY TULLOCH'S SHETLAND

BOBBY TULLOCH'S
SHETLAND

M

MACMILLAN
LONDON

The author would like to thank John Marsden for reading and commenting on the manuscript and to thank Jeni Marsden for compiling the glossary.

Text and illustrations copyright © Bobby Tulloch 1988

First published 1988 by
MACMILLAN LONDON LIMITED
4 Little Essex Street, London WC2R 3LF
and Basingstoke

Associated companies in Auckland, Delhi, Dublin, Gaborone, Hamburg, Harare, Hong Kong, Johannesburg, Kuala Lumpur, Lagos, Manzini, Melbourne, Mexico City, Nairobi, New York, Singapore and Tokyo

Reprinted 1988

British Library Cataloguing in Publication Data
Tulloch, Bobby
    Bobby Tulloch's Shetland.
    1. Natural history—Scotland—Shetland
    I. Title
    574.9411'35 QH141
    ISBN 0–333–45673–4

Typeset by Wyvern Typesetting Limited, Bristol
Printed in Hong Kong

Previous pages *The uninhabited little islands near Scalloway, home to otters, seals and a wealth of birds.*

CONTENTS

Introduction

'You've made a proper hash of it, haven't you?' remarked St Michael to God on returning from a tour of inspection round the world. 'Half the world bleeding under Communist dictators and their admirers, civil war in the Lebanon and international war in the Middle East. Even the comparatively civilised countries are bedevilled by drug-runners, spivs and all sorts of rogues, lawyers, architects, financial racketeers, and all the host of self-important, greedy, prestige-seeking bullies and wide boys.'

'Yes,' said God, shifting uneasily on his throne, 'I must confess that things have not turned out quite as I had hoped. But did you visit the Shetlanders?'

'The Shetlanders!' exclaimed St Michael. 'You mean the people who live on those God-forsaken (saving your presence) Scottish islands that you plonked down off the west coast of Britain to make a target for the winds? Surely you can't expect me to chat up people who only speak Gaelic on islands infested by kilt-wearing, beard-waving, bagpipe-playing incomers from the south?'

'There you go,' retorted God, regaining some of his self-confidence. 'You never were any good at your books – that is why you are such a good soldier.' (God is a little out of date with military training.) 'No respectable Shetlander ever spoke Gaelic, wore a kilt or played the bagpipes. Their islands *are* a little windy, but they do *not* lie off the west coast of Scotland. Indeed they only became part of Scotland by a sad mistake made when my back was turned. They should on no account be held responsible for John Knox, though most of them out of politeness have joined one of his churches. You will find that they are largely free from the vices of which you complain. Off you go, and when you are in Shetland do not forget to stop in Mid Yell and pay my regards to Mr Bobby Tulloch. I regard him as one of my successes.'

God, naturally, was right. The Shetlanders are not such good artists as the Renaissance Italians, nor as musical as the eighteenth-century Germans; they do not cook as well as the French, nor sing as loudly as the Welsh. But they are remarkably free from the vices which plague the modern world: the sins of avarice, aggression, pomposity and pride; they feel no need to posture and preach or patronise. They are mostly a fair credit to the human race and get on reasonably in the world to which

Opposite Shags build large, untidy nests from seaweed and assorted flotsam and as the season progresses the whole area becomes very smelly indeed. As if they were a bit ashamed of the mess, the parents bring in fresh vegetation to decorate the edge of the nest. During the late winter, shags develop their handsome crests, which have usually fallen out by the time most birdwatchers visit the colonies in summer. Probably for this reason, many artists depict shags with only a small tuft on their heads. They are present in Shetland the whole year round.

they have been called. It is not an altogether kindly world. Shetland is as far north as Leningrad and in a more exposed, though less frosty, situation. But that does not make it uninteresting. Shetlanders are tolerant, patient and skilful. I was once asked by a shipping firm if I could help it to get some Shetland seamen to join their line. I asked why the company wanted Shetlanders in particular. 'Because they are the best seamen in Britain, they do not fight and they do not spend their time throwing things at the seagulls.'

What will first strike you about this book are the excellent photographs. They need no introduction; they speak for themselves and tell you more about Shetland and its birds than I, or even Bobby Tulloch, can. I want, however, to draw your attention to the text. It is deceptively simple and clear, but if you attend to it carefully you will learn a lot. Bobby, like many Shetlanders, is a lad o'pairts: crofter, sailor, soldier and fisherman. He has also been admired as a ladies' hairdresser. He has ended up living the life he always wanted to live, as a naturalist.

He has an advantage over most naturalists in having experienced at close quarters the impact of nature on men's lives and livelihoods. He does not censure those who shoot seals and otters for their blubber and skin. He does not blame very poor people for the slaughter of the caa'n whales. He does not pretend that otters will not raid a chicken house. He has no degree or even diploma, but he is a marvellous student of nature. He also has that humility which bureaucratised naturalists often lack. He once told me that he had heard that a lady claimed to be feeding a water-rail on bread. He gently suggested to her that she must be mistaken – the bird could not be a rail. She, with usual Shetland courtesy, had just acknowledged 'Well, Mr Tulloch, if you say so I must be wrong', when the water-rail popped out of a dyke and gobbled up some crumbs. Many naturalists would have hushed up that story.

Shag.

I asked Lord Home why Lord Grey, whom he had known well, had such remarkable success in observing and taming birds. Lord Home replied that one reason was his patience and ability to remain absolutely still for hours. Patience is a Shetland characteristic which Bobby Tulloch enjoys. You might think that you have only to go for a short walk on Hascosay to meet all sorts of rare birds. You might think that it is easy to tell a grey from a common seal, or even a whimbrel from a curlew. It isn't so. It takes patience, observation and skill to get the photographs that Bobby has got. Those absurd sufferers from ornithological St Vitus's dance who dash about the country to catch a glimpse of a bird that they are told is rare are rightly called 'twitchers'. Mr Tulloch tells a typical story of one. 'Twitching' is the very opposite to the kind of observation that Bobby pursues.

We are all apt to kill the thing we love. I fear that the natural world can be destroyed almost as easily by being tramped over, scrutinised and 'protected' as it can be by urban sprawl, the relentless ploughing up of moors, the onset of the deadly hand of bureaucracy with its picnic sites and public lavatories. But at least for the present a fine day on Yell is extremely enjoyable. If you can't take Bobby Tulloch with you, at least take this book.

Lord Grimond
October 1987

Prologue
Bobby Tulloch's Shetland

The Shetland Islands are situated in the cool waters of the northern North Sea a hundred or so miles beyond the mainland of Scotland. Lerwick, Shetland's capital, is nearer to Bergen in Norway than to Aberdeen and accommodates about a third of the islands' total population of over 22,000. Shetland – not 'the Shetlands' – is made up of about a hundred islands, of which only sixteen are inhabited, lying roughly north to south and forming a barrier between the North Sea on one side and the Atlantic Ocean on the other.

The relatively warm currents of the great Gulf Stream that wells up and over the edge of the continental shelf to the west of Shetland carry with them nutrients from the deeper Atlantic into the waters round the islands, not only providing a rich supply of plankton so important to the food chain which supports the wealth of wildlife, but also ensuring that, although Shetland is on the same latitude as Leningrad in Russia and the southern tip of Greenland, we enjoy a fairly mild oceanic type of climate in which the sea never freezes over.

Traditional industries of fishing and agriculture had long been the mainstay of the Shetland economy until, with dramatic suddenness, the 'oil era' threatened to disrupt the whole character of island life in the 1970s. The population shot up by several thousands as men were drafted in to be housed in huge 'construction villages' while they got on with building, at Sullom Voe, the biggest oil terminal in Europe.

Sullom Voe is a deep-water inlet which had already seen service as a base for Coastal Command during the last war. From here pipelines were laid underground and under the sea-bed to bring the crude oil from the production platforms sited sixty to ninety miles east and north-east of Shetland. The oil is stored in huge tanks at Sullom Voe before being loaded into the tankers that will carry it by sea to the world's oil markets.

The Sullom Voe terminal can accommodate up to four ships at any one time, each one of up to 300,000 tons deadweight. Not unnaturally, many fears were expressed for the safety of the whole operation, bearing in mind the stormy climate of the northern winter and the ever-present hazards of a rugged coastline. The pollution caused by the *Torrey Canyon* and *Amoco Cadiz* incidents were fresh in our minds, and local authorities, local and national conservation and environmental

Opposite One of the more numerous of the sea-birds of Shetland, the common guillemot starts to visit the breeding ledges in late winter. In early May it lays its single large egg on a bare rock ledge and, although many eggs get knocked over the cliff in the competition for breeding space, this is minimised by the fact that the egg is strongly pointed at one end so that it tends to roll in a small circle rather than in a straight line. Young guillemots leave the cliff ledges long before they can fly, jumping fearlessly from perhaps a hundred feet up, usually at night to avoid predators.

bodies worked together in co-operation with the oil industry to try to ensure that the oil would flow in and out of Shetland without damage to the well-being of the inhabitants or the wildlife of the islands.

In practice everything has gone pretty well. Apart from a freak accident soon after the terminal opened for business, when a spillage of bunker oil into the sea got out of control and caused the deaths of several thousand sea-birds, the oil has flowed up to and past peak production without serious incident. The floodtide of an outside work-force, the congestion of road, ferry and airport are now merely memories, and Shetland has settled down to some of the fruits of association with the oil industry in better roads, amenities and conditions resulting from some skilful financial negotiations.

But there must be no complacency or lack of vigilance, for accidents can still happen as long as oil is flowing through pipelines under the sea or being carried in ships. In islands so justly famous for rich and diverse wildlife, a serious oil spillage into the sea could prove catastrophic. We can only hope and pray it will never happen.

I was born and brought up on a croft near the shore of the east side of the island of Yell, the second largest island in Shetland. My ancestry can be traced back on one side to the time when Shetland belonged to the united kingdom of Denmark and Norway and on the other to a fugitive fleeing from the battle of Bothwell Bridge in 1668.

From an early age I was fascinated by the natural world. The study and enjoyment of our abundance of wild creatures easily compensated for the lack of material pleasures of a wartime childhood. The need to make a living was an unwelcome necessity which forced me to become apprenticed to a baker. I continued in and out of that trade until 1964 when I reverted to my first love and took on the job of representing the Royal Society for the Protection of Birds in Shetland. I enjoyed that responsibility until 1985, when I took early retirement to spend my remaining active years doing what I most enjoy: studying and photographing, in all its endless variety, the natural world of the islands of the north. By its very nature, island life is a practical business, and so I hope to outwit a few more sea-trout and do battle with a ling or two . . . or even a halibut!

I still have much to learn about the lives and habits of our wild creatures and if, in the course of doing so, I can introduce others to the delights of watching a family of otters or the sights and sounds of a cliff full of sea-birds, then that will only add to my own enjoyment of Shetland and its wildlife.

Bobby Tulloch
Yell, Shetland, 1987

SHETLAND

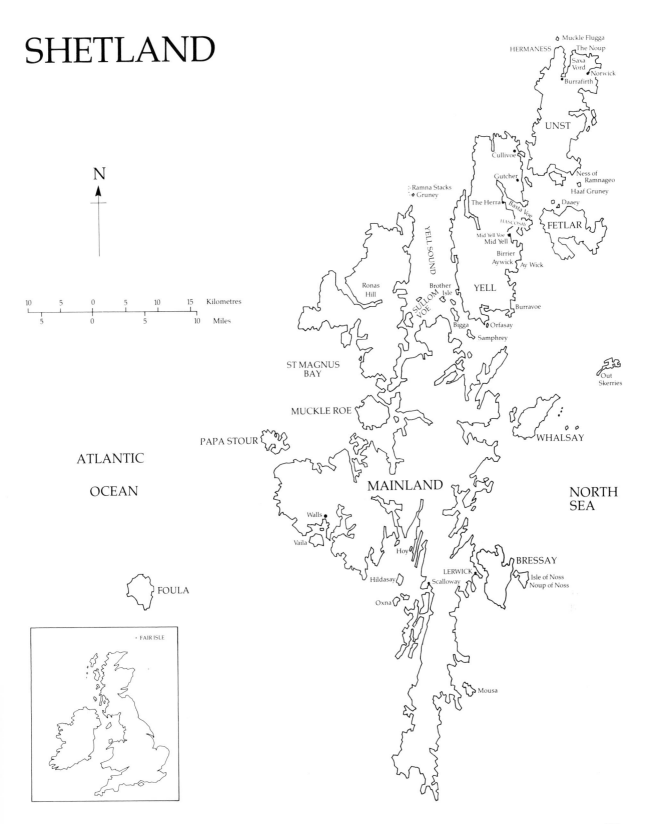

N

| 10 | 5 | 0 | 5 | 10 | 15 | Kilometres |

| 5 | 0 | 5 | 10 | Miles |

ATLANTIC

OCEAN

FOULA

• FAIR ISLE

◊ Muckle Flugga
HERMANESS The Noup
Saxa
Vord
Norwick
Burrafirth

UNST

Cullivoe

Gutcher
Ness of
Ramnageo
:• Ramna Stacks Haaf Gruney
◊ Gruney
The Herra Basta Voe Daaey
HANCOSAY FETLAR
Mid Yell Voe
Mid Yell
Birrier
Aywick Ay Wick

YELL SOUND

Ronas
Hill Brother
Isle YELL
SULLOM Burravoe
VOE
Bigga ◊ Orfasay
Samphrey

ST MAGNUS
BAY Out
Skerries

MUCKLE ROE

PAPA STOUR WHALSAY

MAINLAND NORTH
SEA
Walls
BRESSAY
Vaila
Hoy LERWICK Isle of Noss
Hildasay Scalloway Noup of Noss

Oxna

Mousa

13

Early Days

For at least as long as I can remember I have been interested in the natural wildlife to which I have always had access and, in many ways, even considered myself to be part of.

I say 'at least' because my family told stories about my exploits as a small child of which I have no real recollection. For instance, I seemed to have an affinity with the sea and shore from an early age, often causing alarm by toddling off shorewards whenever parental backs were turned. On one occasion a panic search located me, as usual, near the tideline with a 'prize' in the form of a very dead puffin. Despite my protestations, the stinking corpse was thrown away and I was taken home to be scrubbed and later put to bed. When bedtime came for the rest of the household, my mother looked in as usual to check that I was tucked up and asleep, to be met by a decidedly unwholesome smell. Turning back the bedclothes, she found me blissfully asleep – and clutching once again the dead puffin!

Our life on the croft was frugal, and while we certainly never went hungry there was never much spare cash to buy all those toys which the modern child seems to need for its amusement and education. So, while the puffin incident may have demonstrated a child's need for a play-thing, I think it also showed a certain resourcefulness which may surface in children who cannot have all they desire.

Looking back, I can only admit that my schooldays were enlivened by the advent of the war. My growing interest in looking at and trying to identify every bird which flew past was extended to 'plane watching', and with the Coastal Command base at Sullom Voe only a few miles away, we became familiar with the Sunderland and Catalina flying boats, the Walrus amphibians and the Hurricane and Spitfire fighters which were helping to defend Britain's vital sea links. The real excitement for us, however, was when the silhouettes of high-flying Heinkel and Dornier bombers were recognised, or the sudden dash of a Messerschmidt fighter as it tried to penetrate the Sullom defences.

Previous pages
Shellfish is a favourite item of diet. Razor-shells, or 'spoots' as they are called in Shetland, can be caught at extreme low spring tide. One of my favourite places is Gloup Voe on Yell.

16

The fact that there was sometimes a burst of machine-gun fire – aimed at people, villages, or even ponies on the hill – didn't really concern us kids greatly, only leading to some war games when, armed with wooden guns, we learned the basics of stalking 'the enemy'. When we weren't stalking each other, we stalked the birds along the shores and in the fields or the seals which came ashore to bask on the rocks, and I am certain that the basic techniques we learned in these games helped me a great deal when, much later, I was to re-employ them in the business of photographing many of the animals and birds we had 'shot' with our wooden guns.

Nowadays many people, sick of life in the big cities, opt to live on a small remote croft, seeing self-sufficiency as an ideal for a natural way of living. I can only say that life on a Shetland croft during the last war brought us as near to enforced self-sufficiency as we could be in modern times – and I don't know of anyone who would willingly go back to it.

For one thing, it reinforced the need – so often despised by militant conservationists – to live not only off the land but also, to some extent, off whatever forms of wildlife we had the necessary skills or abilities to procure. I freely admit that, as a boy, I enjoyed the occasional dish of curlew, mallard or wild rock dove, and that we shot the odd seal for its skin and blubber.

Throughout the 1970s, alien shapes began to appear on the horizon as oil explorations gathered momentum. I was born in the croft on the left of this photograph; the firth beyond became a popular 'resting place' for drilling rigs.

At one period during the war, when restaurants in London were desperately short of meat, they were able to offer the rare treat of 'Highland Goose' and 'Highland Duck' on their menus. I wonder how many of their customers, enjoying such delicacies, realised that they were eating gannets and the humble shag which had been shot on the cliffs of Shetland!

The sea has been the background to the life stories of many Shetlanders, and although many of my forebears followed its call either as fishermen or as merchant seamen, I was not destined to do so. Nevertheless, the sea has always had a fascination for me unmatched by any other element and has provided food, relaxation and as much excitement as I could ever wish for.

Fishing has always featured strongly in my life, from small beginnings of stick and bent pin with chewed raw limpets for bait to today's sophisticated sea-angling equipment where a reel costs much more than I earned in a year as an apprentice.

People always say 'The weather was much better when we were children,' but perhaps we only remember the exceptional. I still have vivid memories of apparently endless summer days spent among the rocks and on the beaches, fishing the sillocks as the tide flowed, staying out as the daylight faded and the big pollack came leaping at our home-made flies, or going out in a boat with grandfather and uncles to set long-lines for the haddock and whiting which would be salted down for use during the long dark days of winter.

18

Swimming in the sea was never a favourite pastime. The sea temperature rarely gets much above 10°C even in summer, except where the incoming tide flows over a sun-warmed sandy beach and it can be reasonably pleasant to splash about in the shallows.

We didn't have any sandy beaches at Aywick, but we had our own natural swimming pool. A mile or so from the village a rocky ridge jutted out into the sea and at the back of this ridge, in a hollow in the rocks, was a large deep pool of sea-water, roughly rectangular and perhaps five feet deep at one end with a convenient shallow ledge at the other for the timid. During winter the pool would be scoured by the waves, leaving behind clean cool water which became warmer as the summer progressed.

Apart from occasional groups of splashing, laughing children, the only inhabitants were numbers of three-spined sticklebacks – banestickles we called them. In spring the males are brilliant little fish about three inches long, green and silver above and bright golden-red underneath. The females are a little larger without the red colouring. It is in the spring that the male builds a little nest of seaweed and when the female has laid a quantity of eggs he will guard them closely until the young hatch.

Maybe it was partly for nostalgic reasons that I recently tried to create a rock pool in a fish tank. It was not a great success, but I did get sticklebacks to build a nest and breed where I could watch and photograph them so much better than in those days when we dived in the 'swimming pool' at Aywick!

My three sisters and myself examining a jar of sticklebacks on the shore below our home at North Aywick.

Glaucous gulls visit Shetland in the winter months. They breed nearer the Arctic, in places like Iceland, and wander widely over the oceans in winter, feeding largely on fish and fish offal. Adults lack the dark wing tips found on most of our local gulls.

Winter could bring its own thrills. I learned to watch for the winter birds arriving, the cheerful snow buntings among the stooks of corn, the wild whooper swans which visited the loch, the glaucous gulls which came to scavenge along the shore, and the huge great northern divers which fished in the bay below the croft.

The gulls were not the only ones to scavenge along the shores. Like many Shetland boys, I was an inveterate beachcomber. A sniff of south-easterly wind blowing and we would be off to patrol the favoured beaches, on the lookout for bits of wood, fishing floats, or even for fish which would get flung up on shore if the sea was rough enough, sometimes still alive and kicking.

During the war beachcombing took on a new dimension. Mines would break loose from their anchors and drift around, exploding as soon as one of the 'horns' touched a solid object. Many houses had windows blown out and walls or roofs damaged, and there were even a number of fatalities. Shetland, being completely without 'usable' timber, has to depend on costly imported wood, so not even the threat of being blown up by a mine could deter us from scouring the shores for driftwood.

But it was not just the hope of what I might find that sent me to the shore during a storm. It was the awesome thrill of the storm itself which lured me – and still does. When the wind blows hard over the relatively shallow waters of the North Sea it tends to create a short steep wave of immense power. That water meeting the barrier of the rocky coast creates a scene of unbridled ferocity that few of man's creations can withstand.

Above *Called the 'Rain Goose' in Shetland, the red-throated diver is a summer visitor which breeds on lochs and pools in the peat and heather moorlands. Old people believed that the birds' wild, wailing cry foretold rain. Our grandfather used to say they were calling: 'The more wet, the waar [worse] weather.'*

Right *When snowy owls bred in Fetlar and it was decided to give the public access, building an observation hut without disturbing the nesting birds posed a problem. It was overcome by assembling the hut out of sight and carrying it into position. I am the one directing the traffic, carrying only a hammer!*

Going to school was an unnecessary intrusion into my idyllic lifestyle (or so it seemed at the time!) but there were some compensations. Of the three Rs, reading took first place for me, and the school library made up for all the other boring things our long-suffering teacher tried to get me to learn. Books like *Treasure Island*, *Coral Island*, *The Call of the Wild* and even *Robinson Crusoe* were only temporarily superseded by the Biggles books during the war. But a set of bird books with paintings by artists like Gronvold and Frohawk probably did more to influence me than any other single factor, fanning the already glowing spark of interest in birds. It wasn't long before our small group of real devotees could put a name to almost any bird on the British list.

The village school was a mile and a half from home, with a choice of three main routes to walk. On rainy or snowy days the direct route by road was the best, but whenever we could we followed the stream called the Hogalee burn where we would catch not only the resident brown trout from its peaty water, but in autumn the sea-trout, shining like silver as they made their way up to the headwaters to spawn.

Third and longest was the shore route and on this trail anything might happen. In summer there was a variety of birds' nests to be

Our family croft at North Aywick is situated only a hundred yards or so from the sea, providing a rich playground for bairns. The yellow mimulus or 'monkey flower' is in reality a garden escape, its seeds washing down the streams and drainage ditches.

23

sought out, seals to be seen or, if we were very lucky, we might even meet an otter. We knew many of the wild flowers by name, but not by their English names. Once out of school, where we were expected to show some knowledge of English, we reverted to the dialect of our forefathers, a strange mixture of English, Scots and Old Norse still spoken today over most of Shetland. A great many local names for our native birds, animals, flowers, as well as most Shetland place names, are Norse in origin, a legacy of the long period when Shetland was part of the Norse kingdom.

My home island of Yell is about six miles across and its interior is wild, untouched, peaty moorland where one can still walk all day without meeting a soul.

My first expeditions into that hinterland were made in the company of my grandfather, who liked to spend a whole day every year walking the hills and dales. From him I learned to seek out the breeding places of the bonxie, or great skua, and its smaller cousin the aalin, or Arctic skua. He showed me where the merlins nested on the Kame of Sandwick, the 'shuns' or tarns where the red-throated diver bred, and the overgrown ditch where the wily mallard had chosen to hide her clutch of eggs.

The bonxie or great skua is a summer-breeding visitor which is, in Britain, confined mainly to the northern isles. It lives chiefly by piracy, robbing other birds of fish they had intended for their own young but not hesitating to kill if it gets the chance.

With my father and grandfather. This photograph was taken in the late 1940s.

My grandfather could in no way have been described as a bird-watcher but, in common with so many country people whose lives are spent out of doors, an alert and natural curiosity had brought him a sound knowledge of most of the creatures with which he shared his environment. His practical attitude towards this was demonstrated by the fact that on the homeward part of our yearly pilgrimage he would always be carrying a knotted handkerchief containing half a dozen bonxie's eggs!

So these were some of the influences on my early years which sparked off an interest in wildlife which has stayed with me ever since.

It might be suggested that I led a very restricted life in those early days. There were no bird clubs or natural history organisations that I knew of, no television and little in the way of radio. Even the nearest telephone was several miles away. I had no transport other than my own little legs, though I did get a push-bike when I had saved up the necessary ten shillings.

My dearest possession – though not actually my own – was a pair of old 6 × 30 binoculars which my grandfather had smuggled out of Germany where he had been held in a prison camp during the First World War.

Far from my being restricted, I think the opposite was the case. I knew something of only one island, but an island has a lot going for it. It is defined, unalterable and very satisfying. Others may crave vast prairies, savannahs and veldts. Give me an island and I am happy!

Overleaf *At the latitude of 60°, which is where Shetland lies, summer twilight and dawn are separated only by an hour or so of half-light, which we call the 'simmer dim'. It is often said that on a clear night you can read a book outside right through the night.*

People

After being demobbed from the Army, I went back to the baking trade, but this time on the selling and distribution side. For a year or so I worked in Lerwick doing the rounds with a travelling shop, but then the business in Mid Yell in which my brother-in-law and myself had served our apprenticeship came up for sale and, full of youthful enthusiasm, we took it on.

At that time – the mid fifties – the island of Yell was at a pretty low point economically. We still had no mains electricity, mains water supply or sewage disposal. There were gates to open and close wherever one drove, and tarmac had only begun to appear on the main roads.

Had we possessed any business acumen, I think we would probably have realised that the project was not really viable from the start, but we struggled on for about six years while the buildings, machinery and delivery van became more decrepit every day. Finally it got to the stage where the cash flow could no longer keep up with wages, freight costs and all the other demands, and we had to close down.

I had kept up my bird-watching interests in a desultory way. If I saw anything of interest on my van rounds I would usually stop off and let Charlie Inkster know. The Royal Society for the Protection of Birds had long appreciated the importance of the bird populations of Shetland and had arranged for 'Watchers' to keep an eye on important areas such as Noss and Fetlar, and Charlie Inkster was the Watcher for Yell. Through Charlie I had met George Waterston, who was in charge of the RSPB's activities in Scotland, and on his occasional visits to Shetland I had taken him out in my boat to visit the island of Hascosay, of which he was particularly fond.

It was in late June 1963, just after the bakery closed down and I was rather ineffectually dabbling at lobster fishing, that I got a message asking if I could take George Waterston to Hascosay the next day. I was delighted to do so, quite apart from the importance of earning ten shillings!

At 10 o'clock in the morning we left the pier and chugged out into the voe. It was one of those summer mornings that exiled islanders weep salt tears over: the sun shining from a clear blue sky, the merest ruffle of a breeze to break up the reflection of the green hillsides in the clear waters of the voe, and the only sounds the cry of a tern and the distant wail of a diver.

The cynic might say that there is no greater lover of remote islands than one who doesn't have to live on them, but George had a love of the northern islands so infectious that it penetrated even my own gloomy thoughts on that summer morning. George would have none of it. 'Cheer up!' he said. 'Think of all the thousands of people who are breathing the fumes of the cities, packed into underground trains, or stuck in traffic jams . . . there are so many people who would change places with you that you would be killed in the rush.'

No one could remain depressed for long in George Waterston's company, and I was happy to forget my own worries and let his enthusiasm rub off on me as we wandered over the marshy slopes of Hascosay, listening to the trills of breeding dunlin and watching the amazing aerobatic displays of the Arctic skuas as they evaded the furious attacks of the huge colony of Arctic terns on the slopes behind the long deserted crofts.

Before he left George gave me a hint. 'Don't take on any old job just to earn a little money,' he said. 'I may be able to offer you something more interesting.' My mind ran riot; what could George have in mind? What I didn't know was that there had already been some discussion about the possibility of finding a suitable person to keep an eye on the whole of Shetland on behalf of the RSPB, and that George had already decided I might be that person.

It is not the swallow that is the 'harbinger of summer' in Shetland, but the Arctic tern. After spending our winter in the South Atlantic, even as far as South Georgia or the Falkland Islands, the terns head north to arrive – without the help of clock or compass – on almost the same date each year.

29

A month or two passed and I was beginning to think that George had forgotten me, when a letter arrived offering me the post of Shetland Representative of the Royal Society for the Protection of Birds. To say that I was pleased would be an understatement. The opportunity to follow my hobby – and be paid for it – seemed almost too good to be true. Of course it wasn't all going to be easy. The salary offered was . . . well, 'modest' is a kind word. But I took it on, and in doing so opened up a whole new world of experience.

Part of my job was to be available with help and advice for visitors, particularly members of the Society, and notices were put up in various hotels and places frequented by 'birdy' people to inform them of my existence.

In those days only a trickle of people came up to Shetland in the summer to look at the birds and other wildlife, and I was usually quite happy to be accompanied on my trips, either on sea or land, and to share the experiences of learning more about Shetland wildlife. I had a great deal to learn about people as well as about birds; indeed, 'people watching' can often be more entertaining than birdwatching.

The term 'twitcher' is one which is becoming widely known nowadays. It refers to those people whose main, and sometimes only, interest in birds lies in making and keeping lists of birds seen. They may be world lists, life lists, year lists, country lists or any other lists you can think up. At best this can add purpose and direction to a hobby, encourage people to visit new places, and be great fun. At the other extreme it can be very costly, lead to behaviour which upsets other people, and do little to help promote birdwatching and conservation in general.

It may not be generally realised that birds can be as faithful to their wintering grounds as to their breeding places. This water-rail appeared for a number of years in the garden of friends of mine, eventually becoming so familiar that it came for food when called. The bird probably went back to breed in Scandinavia.

All this was unknown to me when a visitor phoned to say that he had been in Shetland for a week, had only one clear day left and hadn't been able to see either red-necked phalarope or whimbrel. Could I please help? I already had work planned for the following day, but did a mental reshuffle and agreed that, provided he could get to Mid Yell early in the day, it could be done. I explained that it would mean hiring transport all the way (there were no car ferries in those days), but he dismissed that as of much less importance than seeing the birds, and I was very impressed.

The red-necked phalarope is a starling-sized wading bird, a summer visitor in very small numbers to Shetland. In world terms it is not uncommon, but the British population is tiny and confined to the northern isles, so it is a bird difficult for southern birdwatchers to see.

The main population of the red-necked phalarope in Shetland is centred in the north isles, but at that point I hadn't found any in Yell. I knew, however, that phalaropes flew across from Fetlar to feed in a tiny pool on an island a couple of miles offshore. Swimming in tight circles, they stir up insects with their feet, and are so tame and confiding that you can approach to within a few feet and see every detail of this delightful little bird. This was where I planned to give my visitor a real treat.

Above *About 750 species of fungi have been identified in Shetland. Even on the little offshore islands 'horse' mushrooms, such as this* Agaricus *species, can grow as big as dinner plates and can have a fruiting season of up to five months.*

31

The whimbrel is another Arctic species which has a small 'outpost' in Shetland, nesting in small numbers up in the hills. A colony had recently become established in the north part of Yell and we would also have time to visit that.

Next morning the weather didn't look too promising, with all too familiar signs of a rain 'front' approaching, but the taxi bearing Mr Brown (as I shall call him) arrived on time and we set off in my boat.

The weather still held as we approached the island and I was looking forward to the expressions of delight which were sure to follow the first close encounter with the dainty little phalaropes. We were preparing to drop the anchor in the little bay on the south side of the island when I noticed the distinctive, jerky flight of a phalarope flying over towards Fetlar. 'Look!' I said. 'There goes a red-necked phalarope.' Mr Brown swung his glasses round but the bird was little more than a speck. 'Are you perfectly sure?' he asked, and I assured him that it was indeed the bird he had been so keen to see. 'Right,' he said, looking at his watch, 'let's go for whimbrel now.' I explained that we had only to drop anchor and row ashore where he would be able to see the birds much more closely . . . but he interrupted me to say he would rather make all speed back so that we would have time to 'get' whimbrel.

I was speechless. I had never encountered this attitude to birdwatching before and I didn't understand it. I felt quite deflated as we headed for Mid Yell, staring silently through the windscreen which was beginning to be spattered with raindrops. By the time we got to that part of the road nearest to the whimbrel colony the rain had started in earnest, blown almost horizontal by a stiff wind.

The whimbrel is, at first glimpse, very much like the curlew to which it is closely related. The main difference is its call; instead of the well-known 'cour-lee' of the curlew, it has a bubbling or tittering sequence which is very distinctive. As we struggled into waterproofs and gumboots a whimbrel flew past, calling. I glanced sideways but Mr Brown didn't react, and we set out into the teeth of the wind, squelching up to the ankles in the peat hags. After a while I began to feel a little ashamed of my vindictive streak, as poor Mr Brown was showing signs of imminent collapse. Then a whimbrel – or it may have been a curlew – flew across the rainswept moor. 'There you are, there's your bird!' I shouted against the wind, and thankfully we turned back to the car.

Although I felt a little better for having made Mr Brown work harder for his 'tick', I still felt I had wasted a precious day on someone who wasn't the slightest bit interested in the birds themselves.

But with the years has come tolerance, and I now think that one of the great things about this hobby is that it can mean whatever you want it to: a tick on your list, the delight of having a sparrow feed from your hand in a suburban garden, or a lifetime's study of one particular species.

Opposite, above   Red-necked phalarope is a common species in the Arctic but in Britain it is confined to a few select places in the northern and western islands. Arriving back from unknown oceanic wintering places as late as June, the birds get on with the business of raising a family as quickly as possible.

Opposite, below   One of the most evocative sounds of spring in Shetland is the lovely bubbling call of the whimbrel. It is the Arctic version of the more common curlew and, like the phalarope, has its summer headquarters in the northern islands of Shetland.

Overleaf   Surely the most popular of all sea-birds, the comical puffin, with its 'sore feet' walk and nodding gestures, never fails to raise a smile. Puffins arrive on the breeding cliffs in late April and set about preparing burrows for nesting.

The Little Islands

When I was a boy 'going to the isles' conjured up a romantic image almost akin to 'going to the moon'! It always happened in mid-summer and seemed surrounded by an aura of secrecy. Two or three men would prepare a boat with supplies of food, even guns, and disappear for several days. They usually came back when small boys were asleep, which helped maintain the mysterious, and therefore exciting, image. How I longed for the day when I would be big enough to 'go to the isles' – wherever *they* might be.

By the time I had learned the true nature of what 'going to the isles' meant, the whole thing had rather petered out. This was probably just as well because it was really a hunting expedition for seals and birds' eggs.

Seals had long been looked on as a natural resource which could be cropped in the same way as any other. It was only in the 'hungry fifties', after the last war, that high prices for seal skins encouraged too many people to go hunting, to the extent that the population of common seals began to show alarming symptoms of over-exploitation. Fortunately the signs were seen in time and a total ban was imposed on the hunting of common seals. Grey seals had long been protected by restrictions on the numbers which could be killed and, in any case, had never been hunted much in Shetland.

The isles in question were the small uninhabited sheep holms scattered between the large islands of Yell, Unst and Fetlar. It must be admitted that, however romantic my boyhood images were, the isles have been a quieter and better place for wildlife in the last couple of decades than they ever were in the past.

Only two species of seal are native to Britain and they both breed in Shetland. Of the two, common seals are considerably smaller and prefer the more sheltered waters of the voes or the sounds between the islands where they can feed. They also like to haul out on sand or shingle beaches or on seaweed-covered rocks, places which give them good all-round vision – particularly of any humans behaving suspiciously.

A long telephoto lens must look very much like a gun to a seal or bird, and when I wanted to add some pictures of common seals to my library I ran into problems. I had decided that a group of seals which regularly hauled out on the island of Haaf Gruney were the most photogenic and I planned my operation carefully – or so I thought. When the wind was in a certain direction I would land at the far side of the island, crawl across the top and take pictures through a hole in a heap of stones I had arranged beforehand. Everything went as planned except that, when I peered through the stones, the seals were all in the water, obviously alarmed and gazing in every direction. I couldn't understand this; I knew they could not have heard or seen or smelt me, but they certainly knew someone was dangerously near.

I tried again some days later, but the same thing happened. Frustrated, I rolled over on my back to try to puzzle it out and there, hovering overhead, were a couple of gulls. Could they be the culprits? I decided to experiment. Next time I got an opportunity to watch the seals I first went fishing, well away from the seals. Then I went round to the back of the island and began to gut the fish, throwing the offal overboard. Soon I was surrounded by a squawking group of gulls all eager for a feed. I continued until not only the fish guts had been scoffed but most of the fish as well. I then went ashore, trying to give no impression of stealth, and strolled across the island. Only during the last few yards did I drop to a crawl and peer through the pile of rocks. There were the seals, all peaceably ashore on the rocks, many of them asleep without a care in the world. It had worked. I have since used this trick many times, sometimes crawling among the rocks in full view of the seals, which remain unconcerned as long as the gulls are happy.

Taken together, the eighty or so uninhabited islands make up a substantial part of the available habitat in Shetland. If one also takes into account the relative security they offer from land-borne predators, it is not surprising that most of them are well tenanted by birds.

Most of the gull tribe nest on the small islands, and there is usually a pair of great black-backs standing like self-appointed sentinels on the highest point. Common gulls often form loose colonies among the rocks, and black-headed gulls sometimes set up noisy groups on the grass. The graceful Arctic terns, which have flown all the way from the waters around South Africa, prefer to nest, sometimes in spectacular numbers, on the shingle where their eggs are so well camouflaged that it is very unwise to walk on a 'tern beach'. Here and there one may spot an eider, depending on cryptic colouring for its security. The handsome black and white drakes take no part in the nesting duties, but retribution soon follows in the form of an 'eclipse' moult when they turn all black and flightless and go offshore to sulk until, later in the autumn, they once more regain their finery.

Most of the auk tribe – guillemots, razor-bills, etc. – prefer the high cliffs as nesting places, but the tystie, or black guillemot, is the bird of the little isles. Tysties will nest in stone walls, in holes in the peaty soil or even under an old fishbox. Their plumage is shiny black all over apart from a large white patch on each wing, and these formal colours are

Right *Although the glaucous gull normally breeds no nearer to Britain than Iceland, it is closely enough related to our herring gull to enable the two to interbreed. This happened in Shetland a few years ago and the pair here are showing their distinctive wing patterns.*

Below *At peace with the world – an immature common seal basks in the sun below the high cliffs of Hermaness.*

Above *Upholstered by their own fat, common seals lie comfortably on the sharpest rocks and barnacles.*

Left *Common seals can be distinguished from grey seals by their more finely spotted coat and by their head-shape with its 'doggy' profile.*

offset by brilliant red feet. When the bird opens its beak to give its high-pitched call, you can see that the inside of the black beak is also bright red. Most of the auks migrate out to the open seas in the winter time but the tystie stays around the islands through the whole year, merely changing to a winter plumage of mottled grey and white.

Knowing that tysties like to nest well under cover, I decided one year to try an experiment. On the island of Hascosay, less than a mile out from where I live, a group of tysties hung about an area where, to my eyes, there didn't appear to be many suitable nesting crevices. My involvement with the RSPB had taught me all about nest boxes for blue tits and pied flycatchers and how they should be nailed up on trees to provide homes for the woodland birds. How about nest boxes for tysties?

So one fine day in early spring I spent the afternoon humping slabs of rock and constructing a sort of apartment block of nesting chambers, each with a flat 'veranda' for the birds to land on. Tysties have a habit of sitting out in front of their nest entrance, and I could visualise the five occupants of 'Tystie Terrace' calling to each other from the front doors of their superior accommodation.

It was obvious that this would make a nice little story in the RSPB's journal. Since it would also require photographs, I spent another hour constructing a hide from more rocks at a suitable distance from the nest boxes, finishing off the top with a driftwood roof weighted down with rocks to prevent it being blown off by the wind.

Tysties are not early nesters and a couple of months passed before I again anchored in the little geo on Hascosay and went ashore to see whether there were any tenants in the terrace. Disappointment. Not a sign of a bird or an egg in any of the five carefully designed and constructed apartments. Where had I gone wrong? Perhaps tysties chose suitable nesting places in the winter time. Perhaps the group of

Tysties.

Cockersüdies.

birds nearby were all sub-adults not yet ready to breed. Maybe there was some requirement of size or shape obvious only to a tystie. Still puzzling over the reasons for the lack of interest I wandered over to check the photographic hide – and *there*, sitting inside on two eggs, was a tystie!

Although the stone hide got knocked down by the waves the following winter, the nest boxes survived and for several summers were occupied by up to three pairs of tysties before a severe storm washed 'Tystie Terrace' back into the sea.

All the islands are owned or tenanted, usually by a crofter on the adjacent large island, so that even the tiny holms normally have a few sheep to take advantage of the grazing. This means that the vegetation on the islands is kept fairly close-cropped. It is only the few islands without sheep that provide a hint of just how luxuriant the summer flowers can be. Dependent on other factors, including the geology, there are considerable differences in vegetation between the islands. Some may have a carpet of blue spring squill with its lovely scent, to be replaced later by a covering of pink thrift. Others may glow red from miles away with the mass of Shetland red campion, and even those with little soil grow a snowy covering of scurvy grass. On some of the more peaty islands there may be areas of heather and crowberry on the higher ground, enough to encourage a few pairs of dunlin, curlew or even golden plover to breed. Arctic skuas and bonxies may also take advantage of tern colonies or gannet flight paths, often establishing colonies on nearby islands, to make the job of intercepting and robbing passing sea-birds so much easier.

Left *The black guillemot, or 'tystie', differs from other members of the auk family in residing around the coast all year and in laying two eggs.*

Opposite *Herring gull chicks rest beneath red campion, the Shetland form of which is deeper in colour than its mainland counterpart.*

Below *Subjected to wind and wave for centuries, the Shetland coast shows an infinite variety of features. Sea caves abound.*

Arctic skuas mainly live off the Arctic tern. They patrol the terns' feeding grounds in what appears to be an aimless fashion, but should their keen eyes spot a tern heading homeward to feed its own young with a sand eel or young saithe dangling from its beak, the skua changes instantly to a speeding projectile. The tern will try every trick in the book to out-manoeuvre the pursuer but rarely succeeds, finally dropping the fish which the skua deftly catches before it reaches the water.

The bonxie has little of the aerobatic abilities of its smaller relative, but it too lives by piracy although, when necessary, it will add murder to its list of crimes. Bonxies are opportunists and will generally take whatever food is most easily available. Some learn the trick of dashing suddenly past a crowd of puffins, frightening them into flight and usually managing to grab one by the leg or wing before it can get away. Others specialise in robbing gannets, which sometimes have to fly many miles to bring back food for their young. When a bonxie on one of the islands sees a party of gannets heading for home it merely has to fly out a short distance to intercept its victim, usually choosing the last bird of the flight. Interestingly, the bonxies never interfere with an 'empty' gannet going out towards the fishing grounds.

If the gannets are flying low over the water, the bonxie usually overtakes and grabs the wingtip of the tail-ender. A quick upward jerk causes the other wing to hit the water and the unfortunate gannet has to make an ungainly crash-landing. Sometimes the gannet immediately vomits its load of fish and flies off, leaving the bonxie victorious. If not, the bonxie just sits around and every time the gannet tries to take flight, it pulls it down again until the gannet finally pays up and is then allowed to go.

When the gannets are flying fairly high in the air, a slightly different tactic is employed. The bonxie grabs the tail and holds it up so that the gannet, in trying to escape, is flying at a steep angle towards the sea. This usually ends in a spectacular splash – and yet another predigested meal for the bonxie's offspring.

Although I have never seen a bonxie press home an attack on a gannet to the extent of doing it physical harm, they may occasionally do so. They will certainly attack and kill other birds up to the size of a great black-backed gull, especially the recently fledged young which they can easily outwit.

Because of these piratical tendencies bonxies are heartily disliked by many people and there are regular demands for them to be taken off the list of protected species. Certainly in places such as Foula where the bonxies are breeding at a high density, predation on other species must be significant and some form of control may be desirable. But a wider view of the species shows that, though it can be a local menace, the bonxie is a fairly rare bird in world terms. The Antarctic races apart, Shetland has nearly half the world population of bonxies. But point that out to a crofter who has just had his pet duck nicked in front of his very eyes, and you may well be given a new description of the big bad bonxie!

The only potential ground predator on nesting birds is the otter. While I am sure otters will occasionally rob a nest, their favourite food – fish – is normally so abundant in summer that I doubt whether they go out of their way to look for nests or young birds.

Of the many uninhabited islands Hascosay is one of my favourites. Perhaps because it is the nearest to where I live, I have come to know it better than others. I have written of the beauty of the little islands in the summer, but life does not come to a stop entirely in the winter.

Come with me on a fine winter's day with only a thin covering of snow on the ground. The sun is just showing over the hill as we start up the boat engine and chug out into the voe. The light wind is from the north so it will be better to go round and anchor in the bay to the south. Now that it is winter the plankton 'bloom' is past, the water is crystal clear and every detail is visible on the smooth, sandy sea-bed as we drop the anchor over the bows. A group of common seals had slipped off the rocks on our approach and are surfacing downwind of us, nostrils flaring as they try to analyse the strange smells emanating from the boat.

With the engine silent we can hear the 'cal-cal-la-loo' from a flock of long-tailed duck out in the bay. (These ducks are called 'calloo' in Shetland.) Rowing ashore in the dinghy we disturb a party of turnstone on the beach which fly off with their metallic chatter to join a sleepy group of purple sandpiper on the rocks.

After checking the beach for bits of timber or other interesting flotsam, we set out to walk round the ness at the south end of the island. Apart from sheep tracks the snow is smooth along the cliff-edge, but it is not long before another set of tracks can be seen. The imprint of five toes on each foot shows that the tracks were made by an otter. We follow them until they disappear over the cliff, and we can see where the otter has left a long furrow in the snow. I have followed tracks which clearly showed that the animal had gone out of its way to the top of snowdrifts just to slide down to the bottom!

A large flock of great black-backed and herring gulls is roosting on the headland. These are fish-eating gulls which send out 'scouts' to look for shoals of fish. The birds on the headland can tell by the behaviour of the scout when it has spotted a shoal, even though it may be a couple of miles away, and all will fly out to join in the feast.

A flock of shags and a couple of immature cormorants are resting on the grass near the Gunnald. The intense green colour caused by generations of rich droppings indicates that this is a traditional site.

Hascosay once had about thirty people living on it but now only one cottage remains habitable, kept up as a bothy for the shepherd and a

Overleaf *Otters are elusive animals, but a winter covering of snow betrays their nocturnal wanderings. Although getting most of their food from the sea, otters will cross the largest islands from coast to coast in a single night.*

45

place to store the wool clip. Near the cottage a large pool of brackish water is cut off from the sea by a shingle bar. We will sneak up behind the high stone wall and peer over the top. A redshank takes flight with a neurotic yelping; we also put a dozen wigeon and a pair of teal to flight from the pool. There is not much else to be seen except for a small flock of starlings and a couple of ringed plover foraging along the edge of the pool where the snow has melted. A ripple near the bank attracts our attention and quickly we focus our binoculars. An otter dives and surfaces several times, evidently looking for food, then appears with an eel struggling in its jaws. It brings the fish ashore on to the bank and proceeds to eat it, chewing and sucking with eyes closed in evident enjoyment.

We tiptoe away, leaving the otter to its meal in peace. It is time to go back to where the motor-boat is rocking gently on the swell, and make our way homeward as the sun touches the edge of the distant hills.

Many tides have ebbed and flowed since, as a boy, I romanticised about 'going to the isles', but time has not yet robbed them of their magic.

'There's Lingey and Daaey and bonny Hascosay
Oxna, Papa Hildasay and Hoy
Samphrey and Bigga, Brother Isle and Orfasey
Magic names that even Time cannot destroy . . .'

Stacks and Skerries

Shetland is often called 'the land of a hundred islands', and if we define an island as 'a piece of land surrounded by water on which there is some soil and vegetation' then that is about right. But it leaves out an awful lot of lesser islands, which may be grouped together under the heading of 'stacks and skerries'.

Thousands of years of erosion by wind and wave have sculpted this coastline in all its extraordinary variety, leaving dangerous sea-washed skerries and reefs, and lofty stacks pointing like fingers to the sky. Many of them are important for wildlife: seals can find a relatively secure resting place on the low skerries and many sea-birds find nesting or resting places on the ledges of the higher stacks.

My appointment to represent the RSPB in Shetland gave me the justification I needed to acquire a seaworthy boat in which I could visit many of these wild and exciting places which hitherto I had only been able to gaze at from afar. The Ramna Stacks, or Stacks of Fethaland as some call them, were of special interest to me. Not only did they lie in one of the most unpredictable and turbulent areas of tide-torn water round the Shetland coast, but they were known to contain significant numbers of sea-birds – *and* they were owned by my employers. To have a bird reserve within my area of responsibility and not to know how many birds of which species nested there was an embarrassment which I soon set out to remedy.

The Ramna Stacks lie about a mile off the extreme north tip of the Shetland mainland, where strong tidal currents meet and conflict so that even in summer the sea is seldom still enough to allow a close approach, far less a safe landing. In a westerly or northerly gale it can be a fearsome place indeed, as great Atlantic swells combine with tide rips and underwater reefs to set up a turbulence to which all prudent sailors will give a wide berth.

The stacks being twenty-five miles away, the main problem for me lay in accurately predicting the sea conditions. I attempted several trips and was able to get some idea of the bird population on the stacks, but each time the swell kept me from making a landing. At last a large area of stable high pressure produced the conditions which might make a landing possible, and I set out full of anticipation, taking with me a companion to look after the motor-boat while I, with any luck, would be attempting my first ever landing on the Ramna Stacks.

This time luck was with us. After three hours we arrived to find the stacks shimmering in the sun, with only a gentle swell lapping around them and occasionally exposing the fronds of streaming brown seaweed. Fortunately, the geological strata of the area is such that while the west faces of the stacks are near vertical, the eastern side slopes enough to offer hand- and footholds, so that once a landing has been made only a tough scramble remains.

Leaving Johnny to look after the boat, I soon found a likely-looking ledge and, at the peak of a swell, scrambled ashore, pulling the dinghy behind me. The ledge wasn't wide enough to accommodate the little boat so I had to tie it to a projecting ledge above me and leave it dangling.

Soon I was up to the first 'line of defence' where a long row of guillemots stood shoulder to shoulder, crowing and muttering. Youngsters peered out from under the adults, their penetrating cheeps punctuating the general hubbub. Careful to cause as little disturbance as possible, I made my way upwards, side-stepping spitting fulmars, treading with care on ledges slippery with bird-droppings, until at last I stood on the highest point of the stack.

It was a moment to be savoured, and while I got my breath back I looked round at the scene. Way below me the motor-boat rocked gently on the swell and I waved to Johnny who had been watching my progress. Between me and the shore the other stacks stood in a semicircle, while to seaward there was nothing but empty ocean.

Opposite *The offshore stacks provide a useful habitat for sea-birds. The Ramna Stacks are home for many thousands in summer. Remote and rather inaccessible, they have been an RSPB reserve since 1970.*

Below *Soon I was up to the first 'line of defence', where a long row of guillemots stood shoulder to shoulder, crowing and muttering.*

A colony of guillemots high above the sea on top of Fladda, one of the group of sea-washed pinnacles called the Ramna Stacks.

After taking some photographs, I got down to the task of counting the guillemots which almost filled the stack-top gullies and were invisible from the sea. I could happily have spent hours there but, mindful of the turning tide and the other stacks still to be attempted, I made my way back to sea-level.

Two more stacks gave me no more problems than did the first, but the fourth beat me. The smooth grey rock offered no handholds, and as only a couple of fulmars cackled at me derisively from the top I opted to row across to the largest of the group instead.

Unlike the others, this stack has a flat top – hence the name Fladda – with a considerable amount of greenery which gives cover to a colony of great black-backed gulls. These voiced their resentment loudly as I searched for a landing place. A sloping ledge, from which a grey seal flopped in alarm, seemed suitable and, after the usual tussle getting the dinghy away from the sea, I chose a route and headed upwards.

I came to a section of unstable shattered rock which had to be treated with care or a small avalanche might have resulted – which could easily have included me! A number of puffins were nesting in the crevices, but I was too intent on placing my hands and feet to pay them much attention. When I literally came face-to-face with one sitting on its nest, however, I had to get out my camera. Normally puffins nest deep inside burrows in semi-darkness but this one was almost out in the open. It didn't even blink as I took pictures from less than two feet away.

Up on the top of Fladda I was ankle-deep in orache and scurvy grass, with a deafening clamour of black-backs above and half-grown young lumbering off or trying ineffectually to hide in the vegetation. Fulmars sat about, some with downy young, ever ready to spatter trouser-legs with oil. The air was heavy with the musty smell.

I had been specially keen to get on to this stack because I wanted a close look at the cormorant colony. Cormorants are surprisingly scarce breeders in Shetland, mostly nesting on top of inaccessible stacks. I counted thirty-six nests on Fladda, a few still containing eggs but most with young. They were of varying age, from small black, naked reptilian looking objects to gawky fledglings which squealed defiance from cavernous throats as I took photographs.

To my surprise it was now mid-afternoon. So engrossed had I been that I hadn't even kept a weather eye lifted. The tide had changed and a bigger swell was coming up from the west. It was time to go.

A few gallons of water had slopped into the dinghy before I got clear of the rocks, but I was soon back on board the motor-boat, enjoying a brew-up before setting off on the long homeward journey. I was already looking forward to my next visit to RSPB Headquarters, when I could give a first-hand account of the 10,000 or so sea-birds which live on Ramna Stacks.

An off-duty puffin rests at the entrance to its burrow before flying off to sea to fetch more food for its young.

The High Cliffs

The croft at North Aywick is situated a couple of hundred yards or so from the shores of the 'wick', or bay, from which the croft takes its name. Although open to the fury of the south-easterly gales in winter, the immediate shores are low and shelving, providing a reasonably safe playground for children. Immediately to the east, however, and tantalisingly close, the higher cliffs rise up steeply from the sea, topped by a fence to keep the cows from falling over to their death.

This was forbidden territory. Only in the close company of an adult were we allowed to go and look through the fence at the sea crashing on the rocks far below. The lure of forbidden fruit was strong but we had two problems – a short section of open ground separating the safe area from the unsafe, and an eagle-eyed grandmother who kept up an unrelenting vigil whenever we were playing at the 'banks', as the shores are called in Shetland. But little by little, me and my partner-in-crime Danny built up a wall of rocks behind which we could do a belly-crawl across 'no-man's-land', enabling us to reach the high cliffs without anyone realising except our sisters who had been sworn to secrecy.

Oh, the excitement of it all! We climbed down over rocks and grassy ledges which were blue with spring squill. Here the fulmars were sitting on their large white eggs, ready to squirt a mouthful of rancid, smelly oil over us if we ventured too close. Tysties were nesting in holes in the turf, or standing on the ledges watching curiously as two ragamuffins swung perilously from ledge to ledge. The tystie is still a favourite bird of mine. When I walk the cliffs on a hot summer day and the sea breeze brings the evocative – and strangely attractive – scent of fulmar mixed with spring squill, my thoughts wing back to those heady youthful days.

Many years were to pass before I was to realise that our exciting playground of Ramnageo was small beer indeed when compared with all the magnificent cliffs Shetland has to offer; Noss, Fitful Head, Foula and many others were unknown to me. It is on the cliffs and headlands facing the open ocean that the real colonies of sea-birds come ashore every summer to nest, and for me the most exciting of them all is Hermaness on our most northerly island of Unst.

Opposite *Occupying almost inaccessible ledges on the cliff faces, kittiwakes are the most graceful of all the seagulls.*

Opposite *As well as robbing other sea-birds of food intended for their own young, the 'bonxie' or great skua will also feed on fish offal round the fishing boats.*

At its north end the island is deeply cleft by the fjord-like inlet of Burrafirth. To the right as one looks out to sea is the headland of Saxavord, and on the left is Hermaness. According to Norse mythology, two giants called Saxa and Herma lived there and were wont to amuse themselves by throwing huge boulders at each other across the mile or so of water. Apparently some of these fell short, for there is a dangerous reef in the firth called 'Saxa's Baa' or Saxa's Ball.

Hermaness first came to the notice of the early naturalists as one of the few breeding places in Britain of the great skua. Egg collectors had reduced the colony to only three or four pairs by 1860, and the landowner became one of the first active bird protectionists by employing a man to keep watch over the bonxies. This duty was later taken over by the RSPB and the whole Hermaness peninsula eventually became a National Nature Reserve.

Although bonxies are once again numerous on Hermaness, they are far outnumbered by the many thousands of sea-birds which nest in the cliffs and stacks of the headland each summer. Centuries of battering and erosion by wind and wave have formed a coastline which, even without the birds, must rank as one of the most beautiful in Britain.

There have been two new bird colonists in the last hundred years. The first was the fulmar which nested on the Island of Foula in 1876 and spread rapidly around the Shetland coast, reaching Hermaness about 1894. It is now the most widespread – and probably the most numerous – of all our breeding sea-birds.

Below *The fulmar can vomit up foul-smelling oil over anyone approaching, but this one has found a scented bed of sea-pinks to lay its egg in.*

Gannets first came to the Hermaness in 1917. Initially nesting on the outer Stacks, they have spread out to the Mainland cliffs and the colony there is now approaching 10,000 pairs.

The second colonists, the most spectacular birds to nest on the Hermaness cliffs, were the gannets which in 1917 came to Vesta skerry. This is one of the stacks adjacent to the Muckle Flugga lighthouse, Britain's most northerly light. Previously, gannets had nested on the Noup of Noss for a few years, and both colonies flourished to the extent that there are now probably no fewer than 15,000 pairs between the two sites. Much more recently, small colonies have become established on Foula and Fair Isle. The Hermaness colony eventually overflowed from the offshore stacks and on to the landward cliff faces where it still continues to expand.

The cliffs of Hermaness average 400–600 feet round much of the headland, and their upper reaches have grassy slopes which are honeycombed with puffin burrows. Unpredictable birds, puffins have 'off-days' when they all seem to have deserted the cliffs, but on most days they are there in thousands, flying to and from the sea or standing around in groups performing curious little head-twitching rituals.

Along with owls, ducks and a few others, the puffin is a bird which most people recognise. The large, multicoloured beak and funny little growths round its eyes give it a clownish appearance which is easy to caricature. The puffin backs up this image by odd little quirks of behaviour. The head bobbing, beak flicking and 'funny walking' is no doubt of serious significance to other puffins, but it rarely fails to raise a smile on human faces.

Even when newly hatched the young fulmar has the instinct to raise its head and splatter your feet with oil.

The young gannet looks rather like a white teddy bear with a beak, but it will soon attain its adolescent coat.

In its new brown-and-white-spotted plumage, the young gannet wanders widely over the sea before coming back to its base colony at three or four years of age. With its 6-foot wing span, it is among the most spectacular of sea-birds.

Previous pages *Flying high above the sea, the gannets watch for fish. When a shoal is spotted, the birds feed by doing spectacular plunge-dives into the sea.*

For nearly two-thirds of the year the puffin is a bird of the oceans, following the shoals of tiny pelagic fish on which it feeds. Only at the start of the breeding season will it approach land to seek out the burrows and crevices which have been used as nesting places for generations. The single white egg is incubated for over forty days before hatching, and the baby puffin is fed for about the same length of time deep in the darkness of the burrow before it creeps out after dark has fallen to evade the large gulls and skuas. The young bird then joins its parents in a seafaring career until such time as it too will return to play its part in the life of the breeding colony.

Puffins, like other sea-birds, may at times have to travel many miles to find the shoals of small fish on which they feed, and anyone living near a sea-bird colony will be used to seeing a constant traffic of birds. They seem to choose 'flight paths' so that the outgoing birds fly at a different level to those coming back laden with food, and they appear to gain some advantage from flying in groups. These groups may contain birds of several species such as puffins, guillemots and razor-bills, and I have noticed that almost invariably in a mixed flock it is a puffin which takes the lead – perhaps puffins have a 'nose' for good fishing places.

The occasional spurt of earth from a burrow shows that some are on excavation duty. Often they stand around on the clifftop, so unafraid of humans that they sometimes allow themselves to be touched by hand. Small wonder that puffin colonies suffered badly in the old days when sea-birds formed an important source of food for people living on remote islands.

A puffin brings lunch home to the family.

For the most part the cliffs of Hermaness are steep and dangerous, with loose scree slopes and many sudden overhangs, but in a few places there are tortuous paths by which even inexperienced climbers can safely descend to the base of the cliffs. It must be emphasised that none of these paths is obvious from the clifftop and descents should not be attempted without an experienced guide, but anyone who has climbed down regards it as an unforgettable experience. With the sea thundering in the caves and gullies, the forbidding cliff above and thousands of wheeling, screaming, flying sea-birds all around, it is perhaps the most exciting place I know. Here one can sit and watch the domestic activities of the birds with a feeling of being almost part of the colony, so little attention do they pay to a human visitor.

Gannets sit on large bulky nests, keeping a hostile pale blue eye on their neighbours who, although just out of stabbing reach, are always ready to thieve a choice bit of nesting material from the unwary, even though it usually means an acrimonious argument and a clashing of huge 'marlin spike' beaks.

Thousands of guillemots stand shoulder-to-shoulder on slippery, smelly ledges. Every now and then birds rocket in from seaward, small wings beating furiously in last-minute braking as they try to find a parking space on already overcrowded ledges, and causing an irritated

With their relatively small wings, puffins seem to have difficulty in manoeuvering, especially in a breeze.

63

Related to the guillemot, the razorbill nests in smaller numbers, but unlike the guillemot it seeks out individual niches in the cliffs.

braying as they edge into the crowd. The tail of a large sand eel protruding from a beak tells of a successful fishing trip and, like all fishermen, they show off their catch before feeding it to their hungry young.

Their cousins the razor-bills do not usually associate with this common mob but seek out individual niches among the tangle of boulders lower down the cliffs, where they sit with a nose-in-the-air attitude or peer suspiciously out at passers-by. Aptly named, these razor-bills are always ready to slash open any hand that dares to encroach on their privacy.

A shag colony is a smelly, messy place. Although the young instinctively reverse out to the rim of the nest rather than foul their bed, their forcible 'ejection system' usually means that they add to the misery in the next nest down. The adults give the impression of being rather ashamed of all the dirt because they are always bringing in bits of grass and even cliff flowers which they arrange round the edge of the nest.

The overhanging areas of the cliffs defeat most birds, but not the kittiwakes. They place their nests in the most apparently inaccessible places, using moss which they gather from the little streams tumbling over the cliffs. Always happy to be doing things together, they will form a chain of birds between the supply depot and the nesting ledges. Perhaps the most attractive of all our gulls, kittiwakes have a lively, extrovert nature and seem to delight in making as much noise as possible. Amplified by and echoing from the cliffs, against a background of breaking surf, this cacophony is 'cliff music' at its very best.

Other gulls are surprisingly scarce around the Hermaness headland. A few pairs of herring gulls live on the fringes of the gannetry, from which they scrounge most of their food. One of a pair usually nesting on Humla stack is the most aggressive bird I have ever encountered. It will repeatedly strike the head of anyone intruding its territory, hitting harder than any of the bonxies on the hill beyond.

It might be expected that with a large skua colony so near to the sea-bird cliffs there would be constant battles. This is not usually the case, however. It is as if even the bonxies are awed by the sheer number of birds, and most of their predatory raids are carried out on the approaches to the colony where the sea-birds are more scattered.

The auks and gannets bring food to their young from feeding grounds often twenty miles or more from the breeding cliffs, and one of the traditional flyways is through the narrow sounds which separate the islands of Yell and Unst, Fetlar and Hascosay. Bonxies nest on all those islands, and when their young need feeding the parents merely fly out a short distance to intercept a flight of gannets, heavily laden with food for their own young.

However, the bonxie is not always the winner in the game of pass the parcel that ensues. If a fulmar gets there before the bonxie has collected the spoils, it has only to raise its feathers in a threat posture and even the bold bonxie will chicken out, unable to face a beak-full of fulmar oil.

Although man can be made to feel small and even humble in a place like Hermaness, we have it in our power to destroy such bird empires which have evolved over thousands of years. The fish stocks on which the birds depend are also desirable to man, and we now have the technology to wipe out whole fish populations, if international agreements cannot be secured to safeguard their future. Serious damage could also befall the birds should there be a catastrophic accident to an oil tanker or pipeline. That possibility will, I believe, hang over us like a sword of Damocles for as long as oil is being extracted from beneath the sea around Shetland.

Overleaf A line of shags drying out on the rocks after a fishing expedition.

65

The Surrounding Seas

My sisters and I were playing one day among the rocks, near the deep-water Point of Tonga not far from our home. I may have been eight or nine years old, my sisters younger. Suddenly one of them pointed. 'Look,' she said, 'a sail.' A sail indeed; it was the triangular black fin of a sulbregdi, the local name for the basking shark.

We watched with subdued excitement as the fin came nearer and we could see the tip of the tail, unbelievably far behind, sweeping in wide arcs as it propelled the great fish slowly along. Nearer and nearer it came, past the rocks, until we could see the shape of the cavernous open mouth and the massive dark bulk of the body under the water. Our sheepdog Birk – who was also our minder – had spotted the shark and was staring at it with interest, tail wagging. Birk was a real 'sea-dog' who loved swimming, and without really thinking I pointed to the shark and said 'Seek 'im!' Without a second's hesitation the obedient collie leapt into the sea and swam off in pursuit of the basking shark.

Now I had seen these monster sharks before and had learned that they are fairly harmless. The huge gaping mouth is designed to catch nothing larger than plankton and fish fry – but my sisters didn't know that and assumed it was specially designed for eating faithful collie dogs! The ensuing panic was enough to make Birk slow down and, realising he was a bit outclassed, he turned back to be wetly and tearfully hugged.

With our dog Birk, who fancied his chances with a basking shark!

68

Although the thirty-foot-long basking shark was the biggest fish we were ever likely to see, the amount and variety of seashore life was enough to keep us happily exploring whenever we had a chance. The maximum tidal range in Shetland is about two metres, and the very low tides of autumn offered the greatest interest. It was then that the small fish and crustaceans were most numerous. As the great beds of kelp or tangles were uncovered, we would be off to the shore to heave over rocks and wade through the rock pools. Here we would find butterfish, blennies and rocklings, uncover shore crabs, spider crabs and squat lobsters, and watch the spiny sea scorpions change colour to match their surroundings. Hermit crabs were always fun, and starfish and sea urchins an endless source of interest and wonder. Rock pools would form as the tide ebbed and sometimes an unwary fish would get trapped. One well-remembered day I poked at what looked like the leg of a discarded welly boot to find I had tangled with a six-foot conger eel!

Sometimes we would see neesicks – as we called the common porpoise – puffing across the bay, but the occasional sighting of bigger beasts was frustrating when they were too far off to be positively identified. Many years would pass before I was able to go offshore in my own boat, to get a closer look at the whales, dolphins and porpoises.

Several members of the dolphin tribe come to Shetland from time to time. Risso's dolphin is a regular visitor, white-sided and white-beaked dolphins are seen occasionally, and even killer whales call by to put the fear of death into our seals.

Right *A number of species of dolphin are seen from time to time. These are Risso's dolphin.*

Below *Schools of pilot whales often come in to the sheltered voes. Presumably these have surrounded a school of fish or squid and are having a feast.*

Above *Even without man's interference, pilot whales seem particularly prone to becoming beached. Little is known of what causes this.*

Left *As I photographed a school of pilot whales, a group of bulls swam round, keeping an eye on me.*

Porpoises are the smallest of the Cetaceans. They often come puffing round the boat when I am out fishing. We call them 'neesick', which means 'the sneezer', from the sound they make when inhaling at the surface.

The occasional stranding kept up the interest, and even long-dead corpses would be examined and measured and if possible identified. During a south-easterly gale just after the war, a large sperm whale was washed up in the geo not far from our croft. For a while this was of great interest as a flock of gulls gathered every day to feed on the corpse. The problem arose when the gulls, after feeding, flew up to the nearest freshwater loch for a much-needed wash. They weren't to know that the loch was the source of our washing water, and the pervasive smell of decaying whale became increasingly unwelcome. A small mine washed up near the whale offered a solution. We persuaded the mine disposal men to put the object inside the whale before exploding it, and although the geo ledges dripped with rotting blubber for a while, things gradually got back to normal.

In times past a particular species of whale was hunted in Shetland, mainly for the oil obtained from its blubber – the thick layer of fatty tissue which keeps this warm-blooded mammal's body temperature up as it swims in the cold seas. The pilot whale is in Shetland called the caa'in whale (from 'caa' meaning to drive), referring to this docile animal's tendency to allow itself to be herded into shallow water. Up to about the time of the First World War, whenever a school of whales was sighted every available man made for the boats and herded the school on to the nearest beach. Here all the whales would be killed, one-third going to the proprietor of the land on which they were beached and the rest being apportioned out among the hunters.

Today pilot whales still visit our voes and bays on occasion, and have a tendency to become stranded – without human encouragement. Why this should be remains one of the mysteries surrounding the cetaceans; one theory suggests that the animals' navigational mechanism becomes upset by anomalies in the earth's magnetic field.

The largest member of the whale family we see most regularly is the lesser rorqual, called minke by the Norwegians and herring hog by the Shetland fishermen. Now that the large whales have been all but exterminated by the whalers, the minke has become their target. If controls cannot be agreed we are less likely to see the glistening backs of the herring hog in Shetland waters in future.

Overleaf *Two whales from the school beached themselves and died. The reasons remain a mystery.*

Below *A memorable moment when I went up to The Herra to look at a stranded killer whale and found this beautiful adult ivory gull pecking on the carcass. The midwinter light was so bad I had to hand-hold at 1/15 sec to get the picture!*

The Heather Hills

Many thousands of years ago, what is now the North Sea was a vast plain. Mountain ranges rose up to the sky in the east and to a lesser extent in the west and north. Great rivers flowed out over the plains towards the western ocean. As had happened before, however, changes in the climate caused the Arctic ice-cap to expand and all but obliterate much of northern Europe. Again, after thousands of years, the climate reverted and the glaciers began to lose their icy grip. The vast quantities of melting ice caused the sea-level to rise until the great plains were covered in water to form the North Sea.

A hundred miles to the north of what are now the highlands of Scotland, a range of mountain peaks remained above the sea. Rounded and scoured by centuries of creeping glaciers, eroded and sculpted by wind and wave, they became the group of islands which is Shetland. At first barren and inhospitable, the islands were gradually covered by vegetation. With no grazing animals to keep them in check, decaying plants gradually built up on the wetter plains and hillsides to create the peat bogs which now cover much of the islands. The presence of scrubby trees such as birch, rowan, aspen and hazel is indicated not only by remains found deep in the peat, but by relict small trees and bushes still growing today on cliffs and ravines inaccessible to grazing animals.

Man appeared on the scene some five or six thousand years ago and it would not have been too long before he made his mark on the environment. The burning of wood for fuel, the clearing of land for cultivation, and, above all, the proliferation of grazing animals must have had a profound effect on the vegetation and probably hastened the end of whatever woodland existed. Evidence suggests that Shetland has no truly indigenous land mammals and that those few species there are have been introduced, wittingly or otherwise, by man.

Beginning with the smallest, house mice have always lived in company with man, and in Shetland there is evidence that when some of the smaller islands were abandoned by the human population in the last century, it wasn't long before the house mouse also died out. The only other mouse is the Shetland field mouse, found on most of the islands and normally coming into houses only in the winter time. Recent studies by Professor Berry suggest that the Shetland population of *Apodemus* was most likely to have been accidentally introduced by

I had to get up very early to get this shot of the summer sun rising over Mid Yell. The rim-lit sheep adds foreground interest to the picture.

I had to get up very early to get this shot of the summer sun rising over Mid Yell. The rim-lit sheep adds foreground interest to the picture.

Viking colonists, since the mice show genetic affinities closer to those of west Norway than to those of the Scottish mainland. Hill mice, as they are known here, are also interesting in that several different races have been identified. This is an example of 'parallel evolution', where animals living on similar but unconnected islands eventually come to exhibit slightly different characteristics.

The fact that our two species of small mammals are active out of doors only during darkness probably accounts for the absence of birds of prey such as kestrels, short-eared owls and hen harriers. These birds all nest in the neighbouring islands of Orkney, where they prey on the Orkney vole, an endemic species which forages in the daytime.

Next up the line are the black and brown rats. As they are mainly to be found near the shipping and fishing ports of Shetland, we can assume that they originally came in by ship. There is a curious story told on Yell. In the days when the herring fishing was in full swing, about the end of last century, the main village of Mid Yell was infested with rats. One snowy morning someone noticed a strange broad track leading out of

Above *Rabbits have been introduced to most of the islands and flourish even on the smaller offshore isles.*

Right *The red-throated diver, or 'Rain Goose' as it is known in Shetland, breeds on the little peaty pools up on the hills.*

Left *My Mum has been knitting these lovely Shetland shawls for most of her eighty odd years.*

Below *Crofting, particularly sheep-rearing, is one of Shetland's main occupations.*

the village and across to the other side of the island, where it seemed to disappear at the edge of the sea. At the same time people began to notice that rats were no longer to be seen or heard in the houses . . . The following season the herring boom was over and curing stations closed down. While I cannot vouch for the accuracy of the story, I do know that from that day onwards, no rats have ever been recorded on the island.

Another story is told of the stoat, or whitret as it is called locally. Long ago, when the Scottish kings ruled the northern isles, falconry was a favourite royal sport. Each year the King would send his chief falconer to Shetland to collect young peregrine falcons, which meant a stay of a week or two in the islands. In order to feed the captive birds a levy of a chicken per crofter was imposed. One crofter was imprudent enough to try to incite a protest against this loss of poultry and, in order to punish him, the falconer on his next visit brought a pair of stoats to let loose among the man's hens. They are said to be the ancestors of the whitrets so widespread on the Shetland mainland today.

Also confined to the Mainland of Shetland and the island of Vaila are the blue hares which were brought in 'for sporting purposes' as recently as 1907. Brown hares had been introduced about a hundred years earlier but they apparently did not like the country and there hasn't been a reliable sighting still since about 1937. Blue hares thrive, and in their white winter coats are very conspicuous against the dark brown hills.

Hooded crows make amusing and interesting pets, but their mischievous, thieving nature is liable to lead them – and their keeper – into trouble.

Hedgehogs were introduced to Shetland sometime between the wars. Occasionally one finds an albino such as this one, lacking any colour pigment.

Rabbits are numerous all over Shetland although myxomatosis, introduced in the 1950s, periodically wipes out whole communities. As rabbits were introduced to Britain in the twelfth century, we can assume they were brought to Shetland some time after that.

The only other land animal to mention is the hedgehog, said to have been brought in about the middle of last century. Hedgehogs certainly flourish on most of the inhabited islands, and there is an albino strain in the Vidlin area of Mainland. The hedgehogs probably hibernate for about three months in Shetland.

The uniform colour and bare roundness of the hills may give the impression that there is not much variety in the upland vegetation, but this is certainly far from the truth.

The further north, the lower the altitude at which alpine plants grow, and Shetland, at 60° north, has some plants growing on the hilltops which are only to be seen much higher up in the Scottish mountains. For instance on Ronas Hill, our highest at 1475 feet, you will find alpine lady's-mantle and the lovely mountain azalea as well as some of the rarer berry-bearing plants. Blaeberry, cowberry and red bearberry grow on a number of hilltops, as does the smallest of all our 'trees', the least willow. In the heather-covered lower slopes and hills, a really close look could reveal that odd little orchid the lesser twayblade, and the even rarer bog orchid may be seen in the wetter areas. I often make a special early spring visit to the Northmavine area just to see the beautiful purple mountain saxifrage flowering bravely in the cold rocks.

The edible crowberry is found all over Shetland, and you can tell when the berries are ripe because the droppings of hooded crows and the lips of children turn purple!

Above *Shetland hay meadows such as this one at Burrafirth in Unst can show a great variety of colour and of flower species.*

Opposite *On a barren, serpentine-strewn hillside in Unst, Edmonston's chickweed, a native unique to Shetland, shows its white flowers.*

Plants which like wetter conditions include, to name but a few, the curious, insect-eating sundew, the waving white fields of bog cotton and, gracing the peaty pools, the beautiful bog bean.

I always enjoy a visit to the island of Unst. Even though the channel which separates it from Yell is less than a mile wide, the two islands are very different in character, all due to their different geology. Yell is composed largely of gneiss and schists, with a blanket covering of peat. Unst has a greater variety of rocks, and while there is some peat on the Hermaness headland on the west, the east side is largely of serpentine and metagabbro with rocky outcrops, screes and thin but fertile soil. Here on a barren-looking hillside, now a National Nature Reserve, some flowers grow which are found nowhere else in Shetland. The small white flowers of Norwegian sandwort and northern rock-cress can be seen among the startling pink clumps of moss campion, and several species of orchid including fragrant and frog orchids. But pride of place goes to our only unique plant, the Shetland mouse-ear chickweed. This is a variety of the Arctic mouse-ear chickweed and was discovered by an Unst naturalist called Edmonston in the last century.

Merlin nest on the hillsides, mainly using old crows' nests. This is a young bird waiting to be fed.

It is frustrating to be interested in both flowers and birds because of the difficulty of looking up and down at the same time, but at least when you are plant hunting on the hills you can listen for the birds: the plaintive whistle of a golden plover, the trilling of a dunlin or the distinctive songs of curlew and whimbrel. Hear too the weird wail of the red-throated diver as it greets its mate flying in from the sea with a fish. Skuas nest upon many of the higher hills and there is entertainment in the fantastic aerobatic displays of the Arctic skua as it tries to drive its larger cousin, the great skua, away from its territory. You will soon know when you are encroaching on the breeding territory of a bonxie! They are big, bold and quite willing to press home a 'dive-bombing' attack to the extent of bouncing off your head. However, a stick held above the head is usually an adequate deterrent.

Let us not forget the little birds. Skylark, meadow pipit and wheatear are all birds of the hills, and if you hear a sweet 'twangy' song, near the bank of a stream perhaps, look for the twite, our only representative of the finch family.

Apart from the wildlife, just to walk the hills on a fine day can be therapeutic and satisfying. You will rarely meet another soul, and to take your ease by the banks of a tumbling burn, with no sound other than the songs of skylark and curlew, is a refreshing antidote to the stresses and strains of the modern world.

From Hairst
to Hogmanay*

Mushrooms appearing in the fields are a sure sign that summer days are numbered. Several species of edible mushrooms can be found each year, sometimes in large numbers. Their culinary use seems to have been largely ignored until fairly recent times, however. A few years ago a study of the Shetland fungi was begun and well over 700 species have already been identified, several of them new to Britain. Some of the most obvious fungi belong to the group *Hygrocybe*, containing red, orange, yellow, white, even green and pink toadstools. They favour dry grassy slopes and their edibility varies, though the butter mushroom, *H. pratensis*, is quite good.

Different kinds of fungi need different habitats. Closely grazed cliff tops and headlands often have bluets, either the blue-leg or the wood bluet – though there is nothing of the woodland about a salt-swept clifftop. It might be thought that the absence of trees would mean the absence of those species of fungi which can only grow in association with certain trees. To some fungi the creeping willow on the low ground and even the tiny least willow of the hilltops are trees, and woodland species can be found towering above the 'forest' of tiny willows. One fungi which certainly attracts attention whenever it appears is the giant puffball. Specimens with a girth of nearly six feet have been found.

The equinoctial gales can blow with great fury in autumn, battering the shores with huge waves and causing problems for seafarers. This is when the grey seals give birth to their young on the sea-washed beaches below the high cliffs. If a storm should spring up during the first two or three weeks after the birth of the pups, mortality can be high as the helpless pups are swept out to sea or dashed against the rocks. Most Shetland colonies of grey seal are difficult of access, being either below the high cliffs, in sea caves or on offshore rocky islands, but if a visit can be arranged it is a worthwhile experience.

A typical nursery will be a boulder beach where the white-coated pups are scattered, some asleep, some scratching and some busily suckling. Several bull seals will be snorting and splashing, quarrelling and fighting in the surf. Untended pups will be crying and moaning and the mothers might be waving flippers and singing a warning at each other to 'keep off my patch'.

*From Harvest to the New Year.

Overleaf *Winter storms can lash the coastline with great ferocity in winter, making life difficult for humans and animals alike.*

Even on the most wind- and salt-swept headlands different types of mushroom grow. These bluets make delicious eating.

Although the young pups look soft and cuddly, they can be aggressive and their milk teeth are as sharp as needles. Bulls are always busy guarding their 'harem' of cows against the amorous attentions of unmated males and, should one decide he doesn't like the look of you and start lumbering up the beach, don't hang around to shake flippers. A big bull grey seal can weigh up to 900 pounds!

For three or four weeks the young seals stay on the breeding beach, being guarded and fed by the female. Seals' milk is ten times richer than cows' milk, and the pups put on weight at a rate of over three pounds a day until they are so fat they can hardly move. Then, at around three weeks old, they moult their white furry coat and begin to look more like the sleek adults. Females are steely grey above, shading to creamy below, and spotted all over with a darker colour. Males are usually dark grey or brownish with some paler blotches.

Grey seals are great wanderers, and for the first five or six years the young may go off to other countries around the North Sea before returning to their birthplace to breed.

Autumn is the time of 'all change' in the bird world. Out go many of our summer visitors, their place being taken by others from further north. Bonxies and Arctic skuas may keep company with pomarine and long-tailed skuas from the Arctic, and go off to the south Atlantic to harry whatever birds they find there. Birds such as whimbrel, golden plover and dunlin, whose calls enlivened the summer hills, may stay on in Britain, moving to more southerly coastal estuaries such as Morecambe Bay. Our wheatears and the odd pair of nesting swallows may spend the winter catching insects in tropical Africa. Although storm petrels ringed in the Shetland cliffs have been recovered on the coast of South Africa, it is the Arctic tern which is the renowned long-distance traveller. These nimble birds leave our shores to follow the sun to the southern hemisphere for the winter, thus spending their lives in an enviable perpetual summer.

Meanwhile the place of the summer birds is being filled by winter visitors from the less hospitable Arctic regions. Our resident gulls are joined by the big white-winged glaucous gulls from Iceland, and the Iceland gulls from Greenland. (If that sounds odd, blame it on whoever gave the birds their English names!) Most of our red-throated divers move out of Shetland waters, and their place is taken by the great northern divers who will have raised their young on lakes in the Arctic tundra. That smallest of the auks, the little auk, comes all the way from Spitzbergen or Bear Island to take the place of our puffins who have moved offshore to winter in the North Sea.

Many wildfowl also come to Shetland for the winter. Goldeneye, tufted duck, pochard, wigeon and teal are all hurrying away from the onset of the Arctic winter. The majestic whooper swans are familiar and welcome visitors to our freshwater lochs. As soon as their young are

Grey seals choose the most storm-tossed and wave-swept headlands to rear their pups. This is a big bull, who will challenge anyone, human or animal, to approach his harem.

strong on the wing, they will leave their breeding grounds in Iceland to fly back to familiar wintering places. One whooper swan, wintering on the island of Whalsay, flew into overhead wires and was killed; its mate never again left the island, where it lived for twenty-two years until accidentally run over by a car.

Thanks to the Gulf Stream, winters in Shetland are not particularly cold, though the wind may often make it seem so. Snow tends not to lie for long and the sea very rarely freezes. But at 60° north, mid-winter days are short and birds must be able to feed intensively if they are to survive the long dark nights. Farms and crofts provide food for some birds; normally shy rock doves will join starlings, sparrows, blackbirds and even snow buntings in the stackyards where an abundance of seeds can be found. The stubble is foraged by curlew and rooks, and water rails from Scandinavia will join snipe to feed in the wet ditches.

When the ground is snow-covered many of these species will join the rock pipits and wrens to forage among the seaweed on the shores. The intertidal shoreline is a lifesaver because it never freezes, and many insects and crustaceans live among rotting seaweed on the tideline. Wintering waders spend all their time on the shores. Turnstones have evolved the trick of turning over pebbles to catch little crustaceans such as sand-hoppers. The purple sandpiper, that most self-effacing of waders, lives quietly on the rocky parts, while the excitable, all-seeing redshank seems to be a self-appointed watchdog.

Whooper swans, and ducks such as the tufted duck, will stay on the freshwater lochs for as long as possible before moving on to the sea in freezing weather.

In winter, snipe feed in the marshes and on the wet ground. They too will go to the seashore when the ground gets frozen.

Though time may be short, birdwatching on a fine winter's day can still be exciting, with a variety of rare Arctic birds to be seen. The flocks of cooing eider duck and yodelling long-tailed duck must be checked in case they have been joined by a majestic king eider. Is that distant diver really a great northern or does the pale beak suggest a white-billed diver, the rarest of all the divers? The gull flocks must also be examined in case a pink-breasted Ross's gull or a snowy-white ivory gull has decided to pay us a visit.

Offshore where the fishing boats tow their seine nets and the fish are gutted at sea, gulls and fulmars can make a very good living. They feed even at night by the light of the boats.

Ashore, too, the scavengers don't do badly. Modern man is a wasteful animal, and refuse tips are picked over by gulls, crows and ravens. Fish and shellfish processing factories also dump offal where these species can find a meal.

Another source of food, especially for crows and ravens, are the hill sheep which fail to survive the winter, or the road casualties, mainly rabbits and the occasional sheep. Many people despise the crows and ravens, but one has to acknowledge their ability to survive in the face of adversity. Having kept crows as pets when I was a boy, I learned just how clever they can be. Mischievous and thieving they certainly were and got me into trouble often enough, but I like them still. They were part of my upbringing and the environment I enjoyed then and still do today.

Someone once asked me which season I liked best. 'Next season' was the only answer I could think of.

Shetland Seasons

The hanging up of new calendars, the greetings and resolutions which herald a new year, all have a strong psychological effect upon the human population, kidding us into a belief that the worst of the winter is past and that spring is just around the corner.

Alas, there is no such uplifting of spirits throughout the natural world, and for many, the worst is yet to come. The fat – and therefore energy – resources laid on during the bounteous months are becoming more meagre now, and for many birds and animals it will be a race against time. The whole system is finely tuned towards survival, and in average conditions those species which are resident on the islands will come through in sufficient numbers to carry on the race.

The wren is a good example of this; the fact that wrens have lived in Shetland long enough to have developed racial features sufficiently distinct for them to be measured and recognised by us, means that they have been with us for a long long time. But it is also obvious that when we get a winter with a particularly extended spell of frost and snow, the wren population can be decimated, and it may be several years before that lovely defiant song can again be heard above the strongest gale.

Just as humans have developed languages and dialects through living in relative isolation, wrens (and other resident species too) have acquired their own song phrases peculiar to the various local races.

On one of my first visits to Fair Isle, with senses all tuned up to finding rare and exotic birds, I leapt up from the breakfast table on hearing an unfamiliar bird song, to find it was only a Fair Isle wren on the garden fence. I got some funny looks from the assembled bird-watchers as I sheepishly resumed my place at the table, muttering something about Fair Isle wrens not speaking Shetlandic.

Many years later on another lovely island, Hirta in the St Kilda group, I was again conscious of a different wren song, this time I suppose it was the avian equivalent to singing in Gaelic!

As we have no mountains in Shetland and, due to the Gulf Stream, a fairly mild surrounding ocean, prolonged snow and really hard frosts are rare in Shetland, enabling many birds and animals to stay the whole year round. But there is an important limiting factor: the metabolism of many birds – more so in the smaller species – is such that they need to feed at fairly frequent intervals, and the physical situation of Shetland is such that we have at least sixteen hours of darkness in midwinter. This, and the scarcity of active insect life at that time, rules us 'out of bounds' to small birds such as warblers during the winter.

But a surprising number of birds do manage to survive the Shetland winter. Although familiar and popular in English gardens, the robin is absent from Shetland as a breeding bird (in fact there is no record of a British robin ever having visited Shetland, as far as I know) yet during many winters almost every croft stackyard, manse garden and little plantation of bushes will have a resident robin. These are probably birds from the northern part of Scandinavia where conditions are just too extreme for the birds' survival.

When the old Julian calendar was replaced by the Gregorian calendar in Britain in 1752 and eleven days were 'lost' in the transition, many of the more remote parts of the country refused to accept the change. Shetland largely resisted the change and today there are still a few outlying townships who celebrate 'Old Yule' on the 5th (or 6th, depending on where you live) of January, and 'Old Newerday' a week later. There is a saying that the day is a 'cock's stride' longer at Old Newerday, even if the 'hardest' part of the winter is probably yet to come.

The first stirrings of spring can be detected during February. Ravens will be displaying and repairing nests high up on the cliff-faces, and by the end of the month gannets will be returning to quarrel and fight over the remains of last year's nests which have survived the winter gales.

It is not unusual, if the month of February is mild, to get reports of blackbirds nest-building and skylarks starting to sing, but the old folk are suspicious of a too mild February; 'There'll be a cooling yet' they prophesy, and they are usually right. There is often a spell of bitter northerly winds around mid-March, and the skylarks which were singing blithely will be huddled in small flocks on the stubble while a blizzard of snow puts a temporary end to thoughts of advertising for a mate.

This is the period when otters are most active; most females come into 'season' and males are constantly on the go, checking out all the markers of scented 'spraints' around the perimeters of their chosen territory.

Short sharp encounters between rival males are not uncommon. A neighbour of mine who lives near the sea was startled at breakfast one morning to hear sounds of an altercation, and there just outside the kitchen window a couple of otters were having a squealing row while a third – probably a female – was sitting nearby calmly looking on!

Although there are records of April blizzards, we normally expect to see real signs of the approaching summer. A few flowers will be opening their petals to the strengthening rays of the sun; a sprinkling of daisies will appear in the fields and the yellow stars of lesser celandine

Overleaf Herons from Scandinavia will spend the whole winter in the more sheltered voes and along the shore.

will add a splash of colour to sheltered slopes. Lapwings and golden plovers will have returned to their chosen territories in the fields and hills, early mallard will be sitting on well hidden clutches and the cliff ledges will be crowded with guillemots and razorbills. Puffins arrive inshore towards the end of the month, but are not usually ashore in any number until well into May.

A lot of bird activity passes unseen during April as returning migrants fly over to their summer homes in Scandinavia. It is only when bad visibility and east or south-east winds blow them off course that many will be forced to drop in on Shetland to rest and feed until favourable conditions allow them to continue their journey to their summer home.

Typical early migrants will be parties of chaffinch and brambling heading for the Norwegian forests, or perhaps it might be a 'robin year' when they will move through in their thousands. Sometimes the urge to establish territories is already strong and males will proclaim ownership of a croft garden by singing constantly for a few days before moving on.

It is obvious that some element of chance is involved, because in years when there has been a strong spring migration a few birds will stay on to nest in Shetland, adding species like white wagtail, chaffinch, goldcrest, fieldfare, redwing, blackcap and even reed warbler. Nineteen seventy-three was such a year, and a pair of reed warblers actually nested successfully – the only breeding record for Scotland.

Late April and early May are the great spring change-over times. All our breeding visitors will have arrived, except red-necked phalarope, which will show up later in May. Arctic terns will be on cue from 6 May, Arctic skuas to annoy them having arrived during the last week of April, and so on.

At the same time the wintering birds slip away unseen; the whooper swans and great northern divers to their breeding marshes and lakes in Iceland and beyond, turnstones and purple sandpipers, snow buntings and redpolls also returning to the Arctic, sometimes leaving the odd pair to stay on for the summer to get us all excited in case they provide us with a new breeding record.

I used to find that working for the RSPB was eleven months of preparation and one of frantic work, because in Shetland wildlife terms everything happens in June. The days have lengthened to the stage where there is literally no night, only the brief so-called 'simmer dim' when things quieten down for an hour or two before the sun re-appears. Dawn chorus at 2 a.m. can get a bit wearying after a while.

I have written elsewhere about the summer scene of intense activity when you would like to be in ten places at the one time, but it is short-lived. Early July sees the first exodus take place, when the young guillemots leave the cliffs, to be followed by the puffins and finally in early September by the bulk of the gannets, leaving the trampled nests and whitewashed ledges to the cleansing power of the autumn gales.

Now I feel the same about autumn, perhaps because of a sense that it is all over for another year, and nature is relaxing. It is time to catch, salt and freeze fish for the winter – most of what I catch to salt away is ling, saithe and tusk; to arrange for a tasty heather-fed Shetland lamb or two which can be salted and frozen, or 'reested', that is salted and hung up above a peat fire to take on that lovely distinctive flavour from the smoke.

Peat, there's another thing. In former times many of the fine days of summer had to be spent cutting, curing and bringing home the winter fuel. Recent developments in mechanical technology have meant that those of us who find the peat work a chore or who aren't physically able for the hard labour entailed can arrange to have our winter supply of peats delivered to the doors of our peat sheds. Of course there's not much other fuel to use on the islands – very few trees as it is so far north, and no coal unless it is imported.

It is easy to keep a log of bird arrivals, but not easy accurately to detect departures. When *did* I last see an Arctic skua? Oyster-catchers also have gone, but when?

It seems only a week or two since there was a magnificent great northern diver in full breeding plumage in the voe. I wonder if this is the same bird back again, now moulting into winter dress and with a youngster following it everywhere?

Overleaf *Occasionally a small offshore island has no animals to graze the vegetation, and only then can it be seen how colourful the islands would be without sheep.*

A rare sight indeed – an almost pure white puffin.

November can be a pleasant month in Shetland. With the equinoctial gales past, settled weather can allow the grey seal pups to lie up safely on the exposed beaches below the high cliffs. The late autumn vegetation and the insect life in the stubble and potato fields have helped sustain the flocks of fieldfares and redwing – and wasn't that White's thrush a cracker!

The waxwings have had the last of the rowan berries and have moved on. My neighbours report that 'their' water rail has arrived yet again.

Last night I went out for a look at the sky before going to bed and, as I have done many times before, gazed in wonder at the aurora borealis. The 'merry dancers' they are called in Shetland. There was an arc of intense darkness above the northern horizon, and above that curtains of wavering light, now red like the glow from a distant fire, now blue like a glacier. Changing shape and colour with breathtaking speed, it was easy to believe the people who swear they have heard a sound 'like rustling silk' emanating from the aurora.

It was difficult not to be affected by the sight of such remote, untouchable magnificence. Easy to reflect on the power of nature and the insignificance of man, and to forget the poisons we pour into the oceans and into the atmosphere. Man has no right – far less a God-given right – to destroy a single species on this earth, yet we are forever attempting to do so, and all too often succeeding.

The 'merry dancers' flickered and faded. The show was over. I shivered and noticed that the air was quite chilly. The aurora often seems to foretell a cold spell and, after all, it is winter again. Full circle, another year older, and where did it all disappear to so quickly?

Of Seals
and Snowy Owls

Just as every angler dreams of catching the 'big one' that beats the world record, and the stamp collector dreams of finding a Penny Black in a dusty old box, so one of my boyhood fantasies was of discovering the nest of some rare and exotic bird. Perhaps it would be a great northern diver on some secret hill loch to which I would take a small select group of friends, only after they had been sworn to secrecy. Little did I know that one day something very like this would actually happen, although the results were not quite those I had envisaged.

The snowy owl is an Arctic bird, normally found on the tundra belt beyond the treeline in places such as Canada, Siberia and northern Scandinavia. Snowy owls had only been recorded as vagrants to Britain, and a few of these may have escaped from zoos, where they can be bred. Their principal food is the lemming, a mouse-like rodent of the Arctic which is known to suffer periodic population changes. Years of abundance are followed by a 'crash', and during the following lean years predators such as the snowy owl may wander more widely in search of food. One such year of shortage probably occurred in 1964, because one or two snowy owls turned up in Shetland – the first I had ever seen. Most of the reports were of the pure white male birds, although a brown spotted female was recorded in Fetlar in the winter of 1966.

This then was the background to that memorable day in June 1967 when I took a party of Swiss birdwatchers over to Fetlar in my boat to look at the whimbrel and red-necked phalarope.

We landed in the bay to the north of the island and walked up the hill through the ruins of the deserted township of Russetter, where the party were delighted to see breeding common sandpipers, redshank, oystercatchers and lapwing. Up on the drier slopes of the rocky hill of Stakkaberg we stopped to savour the song of whimbrel and the piping of golden plover. One of the ladies tugged my sleeve. 'What is that bird?' she whispered, pointing to the top of the rocky ridge. I swung my binoculars and there was a magnificent male snowy owl sitting on a rock, glaring at us with great yellow eyes. This was a real bonus, as there hadn't been any reports for quite a while. Eleven pairs of binoculars took in every detail of a bird none of the visitors had expected to see in

101

Left *The first brood of snowy owls ever to have hatched in the wild in Britain on the island of Fetlar in 1967.*

Opposite *A young snowy owl sits in the lee of a rock waiting to be fed. When full grown, it will have a wing spread of nearly 5 feet.*

Below *A young male snowy owl which has had a damaged wing trying out his wings after recovery.*

Mother snowy owl watches intently as her chick tries to swallow a large piece of rabbit. The male bird did all the hunting and rabbits were the main food during the nine years that they bred on Fetlar.

Shetland. But I was puzzled by the owl's behaviour. Normally during the day snowy owls sit hunched in the lee of a rock looking supremely bored. This one was on top of the rocks looking aggressive.

On the pretext of looking for owl pellets, those indigestible food remains regurgitated by birds of prey, I left the party and moved round the back of the rocks behind the bird. Suddenly a female owl flew from a hummock and there, in a little hollow, were three white eggs. My immediate inclination was to rush back and tell everyone what I had found, but I forced myself to think of the implications. Here was an event unprecedented in British ornithological history which would send birdwatchers – and possibly egg collectors – hot-foot to Shetland as soon as the news broke. The nest was on the ground only twenty minutes' walk from the public road, where it just wouldn't stand a chance.

The Swiss party was leaving the next day to tour Scotland. I couldn't take the risk, and forced myself to stroll casually back, saying 'No, I didn't find any pellets.' I must have seemed a bit preoccupied as we ambled back towards the boat and as soon as I could decently do so I left my party and rushed to a telephone. I needed advice and urgent action, and the RSPB responded immediately. Within days a round-the-clock guard was mounted from a hastily erected hut which a neighbour of mine had intended to be his garden shed, and an empty cottage was secured in the nearest township on Fetlar to house the voluntary wardens.

When the press release went out the effect was greater than I had ever imagined. Even the national dailies featured the story, and I was taken to London for a television appearance. As expected, the visitors arrived in droves. They were taken up the hill to look through a telescope in the hide at the now famous birds which, through it all, simply got on with the business of raising their family.

Seven eggs were eventually laid, from which six young hatched and five were reared – a remarkable effort which, although the owls stayed on to breed for nine years, they never again matched. Altogether about twenty young snowy owls were raised and still an occasional owl may be seen on the hill where birdwatching history was made.

Birds, with their power of flight, are able to make these sudden dramatic appearances. For land animals there is no such chance, but those that swim in the sea may turn up unexpectedly from time to time. Several seal species of the Arctic oceans have been recorded in Shetland in the past, and I always look carefully at our seals in the hope of finding that one of these rarities has decided to pay us a visit.

One day my wife, who was the district nurse on Yell at the time, casually mentioned a seal she had seen hauled out on the grass by the roadside in the township of Cullivoe. 'Oh yes,' I replied, 'it will be a sick animal which has crawled out to die.' But when a few days later she again reported that the seal was up on the grass and didn't appear to be sickly, I decided to investigate. Needless to say, when I travelled the dozen miles to Cullivoe the seal was nowhere to be seen.

As I waited in case the animal reappeared, I chatted to a fisherman familiar with the local seals. He reckoned that this one was a stranger. When he described the pale brown body and the exceptionally long whiskers, I began to realise with growing disappointment that I might have missed a bearded seal, possibly the only one to visit Britain this century. As we talked, a dark head appeared above the water and my pulse raced when the curtain of white bristles hanging from its upper lip proclaimed that indeed it was a bearded seal!

Later on, the beast hauled out on to the little jetty and we watched with amusement as the long 'moustache' which had been straight when wet began to curl up at the ends as it dried, until each bristle looked like

the hair spring of a clock. The seal was about six feet in length and we judged it to be a sub-adult male.

A couple of years later, yet another bearded seal turned up. A female this time, it appeared in the voe near our own house and, apart from being smaller, it was just as tame and approachable as the first and also liked to haul out on the grass. After a week or so, it too disappeared as mysteriously as it had arrived.

My work with the RSPB included taking part in population studies and surveys from time to time. A study of breeding terns meant visiting many of the little offshore islands in my boat. The usual drill was to anchor the motor-boat in a suitable place and row ashore in a dinghy. The day I chose to visit the furthest island was fine and sunny, so I slung my camera bag on my back before rowing ashore. As I neared the rocks I looked over my shoulder for a landing spot and nearly dropped my oars when I saw, only a few feet away, a seal the like of which I had never seen in my life. The blue-grey fur of its upper parts was clearly differentiated from the creamy underside and I stared in disbelief as I fumbled for my camera. It had to be a young hooded seal!

The whiskers on this bearded seal are quite straight while they are wet, but as they dry out they curl up at the ends. This seal, which appeared in Cullivoe, Yell, was the first of its species to be recorded in Britain this century.

Hooded seals breed along the edge of the pack ice of the Arctic Ocean, the main concentration being near Jan Mayen island where the pups are born in early April. So this animal was only three months old, confirmed by its size and the fact that it still had its 'baby' coat. The reason I had got so close, I soon realised, was that the poor thing was nearly blind. Presumably it had become separated from its mother and had swum blindly on, living by reabsorbing the thick layer of blubber laid on by the rich milk of its mother. If this guess was correct, it would have needed to average about ten miles a day to reach Shetland. This possibility had already been demonstrated by a young grey seal which turned up on a beach in Unst wearing a numbered plastic tag. The Seal Research Unit at Cambridge confirmed that it had been tagged only two weeks earlier, on the Farne Islands, giving it too a swimming speed of ten miles a day.

One day in the late July of 1981 I decided to visit Unst by car. Just after the car ferry had pulled out from the terminal at Gutcher I went to the rail with binoculars, as usual, to see what birds were moving in the sound. Looking back towards the pier we had just left, I could see, almost in silhouette, an animal lying on the rocks. It seemed to have its hind end tucked underneath. As it receded from view I realised that the only animal in the north Atlantic which could tuck in its hind flippers was the walrus – and hadn't I seen a hint of rusty brown colour?

Without saying a word I stayed aboard the ferry and went back to Yell, heaving a sigh of relief when I saw the animal still on the rock. As we got nearer it was obvious that my guess was right. It was a walrus. It had little six-inch tusks, showing that it was only a baby . . . with an estimated bodyweight of half a ton! Wally became quite a celebrity, with his photograph in the papers. He eventually moved down to Mid Yell and took up residence near a clam bed where he stayed for about a week, so near to our house that I was able to sit up in bed in the morning and check whether he was feeding or sleeping on the rocks.

A walrus, probably the same animal, turned up at various places down the east coast of Britain. I believe it was eventually taken in charge and flown to Iceland. From there it was transported by gunboat and released near the icepack off Greenland. Thus ended an epic attempt at a walrus world tour!

Right *A young hooded seal on Haaf Gruney, the first to be recorded in Shetland.*

Opposite *Half a ton of baby walrus which appeared in Yell one summer.*

Below *A wintry sunrise over Mid Yell.*

Otters

No one knows when or how otters first came to the islands. It is possible that they arrived unaided at some point in the distant past, perhaps when the sea-gap was smaller than it is today. Otters could have been one of the first land animals to colonise successfully after the last ice age. They don't need vegetation and their main food, fish, would have been readily available.

But although otters are capable swimmers and certainly commute between many islands in the Shetland group, I doubt whether they would be able to sustain a long sea crossing. For one thing their fur, dense and waterproof as it is, is not totally impermeable and does become saturated after a time. This is why an otter, after perhaps half an hour's fishing, comes ashore for a protracted spell of grooming. I used to wonder why, after taking so much trouble to get dry and fluffy, they then walk straight back into the sea.

Once the animal gets really wet, it is as vulnerable to hypothermia as you or I, with little subcutaneous fat on its body to help keep it warm. This is where seals score and are able to make really long sea voyages. Their insulation lies not in the outside hair but in the very thick layer of blubber which wraps them round like an immensely thick wet-suit.

Pet or captive otters were known to have been kept by the Vikings and, master escapologists that they are, they probably had little difficulty in escaping from cages or enclosures.

It is also possible that otters could have arrived in Shetland as stowaways. I know of at least one instance where an inquisitive otter had been startled while investigating a boat, and had disappeared into the bilges where all attempts to dislodge it failed and the boat sailed with its furry passenger still on board. On one occasion, I had tied my boat up at an old jetty on Fetlar while I looked at the birds on a nearby loch, and the day being fine I had left the wheelhouse door open. When I got back an otter, which had been investigating the cabin, rushed past me and jumped into the sea.

When the inter-island car-ferry system was introduced a few years ago in Shetland, the landing ramps were given protection from the open sea by building rock and boulder breakwaters. It wasn't long before otters discovered many secure holes and crevices in these which made excellent holts and lie-ups. Nowadays one of the best ways to see an otter is to go to one of the ferry terminals and just sit in the car and watch. The ferries are tied up each night at the ramps and if there happens to have been a snow shower during the night there is often a pattern of otter footprints all over the car-decks the next morning. All the ferry terminals have toilet facilities, and for a time the ladies' loo at Fetlar was regularly used by otters. Let's hope they were lady otters!

Some people say that otters cannot tolerate the human scent and will desert a holt if it is so much as touched by a human, but my experience is almost the opposite. So long as they are left alone otters will live quite happily in regular contact with human activities. I have known many instances where otters have chosen to make their home in byres, barns or under the floors of regularly used sheds. One lady contacted me recently asking if I could suggest a way of discouraging otters from beneath the floor of her garage. The smell was becoming intolerable but she didn't like to block up any openings in case a family were entombed inside.

I first encountered an otter when I was a little boy playing among the rocks on the shore below our croft. I heard a noise and peered round a rock to see what I thought was this big brown cat sitting on the seaweed eating a fish. This wasn't too surprising, as our house cats used to follow us to the rocks and wait for us to catch them a fish or two. What did astonish me was that when I called out 'Puss, Puss' to this strange cat, it immediately slid into the sea and disappeared from sight. I was rather upset about this, being convinced that the 'cat' had drowned, but on telling the story when I went back home, I was laughed at and assured that I had seen an otter which was quite at home in the sea.

The otter who had not learned that it is forbidden to eat chickens.

Opposite *Two otters eating a lumpsucker on the shores of Basta Voe.*

In those days many districts in Shetland had their otter hunter, generally a crofter whose hunting instincts were keen enough to be able to outwit this most elusive of animals. Gun, trap and 'otter houses' were all employed, and the money from the skins was a welcome addition to the meagre living from the croft. Nowadays such practices are no longer necessary and otters are fully protected by law.

In our district a man we knew as 'Shootin' Willie' was the acknowledged otter expert and, with my interest whetted, I took every opportunity to waylay him with questions and to listen to his stories of encounters with 'Dratsie', the otter.

The Shetland equivalent of 'Live and let live' is 'Let be for let be', and this is often qualified by saying 'as Robbie o' the Glen said to the otter.' Robbie lived many years ago and earned part of his living by catching otters. One method of trapping was to build stone 'otter houses' near known otter paths. Each 'house' had a trap-door which fell when the otter, baited by a bit of fish, had entered and stepped on the release mechanism. The story is that Robbie, finding an otter in one of his traps, felled it and set off for home. He was carrying the otter by the tail, slung over his shoulder, when the stunned animal came to life and sank its teeth into Robbie's behind. So there they were, hanging on to each other's tail until Robbie in anguish cried out 'Let be for let be' and they both let go.

Right *Caught at play in a peaty pool on Burraness, an adolescent otter warily eyes the photographer.*

Although that story has now passed into Shetland folklore, 'Shootin' Willie' Thompson used to tell a very similar tale. He had tracked down and shot an otter along the shore past Gossabrough where he lived, and was carrying it home in the same way, slung over his shoulder. Without warning the otter came to life and sank its teeth into the small of Willie's back. His reaction was to fling himself backwards on top of the otter, hanging on to the tail with one hand while he tried to find his only weapon, a small penknife, in his pocket.

There was no question of 'Let be for let be.' Willie was determined not to let go of his prize, and they struggled and thrashed until, locked in a far from loving embrace, they both rolled over the cliff edge. Fortunately for Willie the cliff was grassy and not very high. By the time they came to a stop, the fight was over and the otter was dead. Although 'Shootin' Willie' won the day and got his otter skin, it took a long time before his own skin recovered from the bites and bruises he got in his battle with dratsie.

Another otter story is told about a Fetlar man who had a tame female otter which he kept in the barn next to his croft. When she was in season, she was visited by male animals intent on a spot of courting. Whenever the man heard the sounds that told him his otter had a visitor, he would block up the hole by which it had entered and then, seizing a flail, he would go into the barn and kill the would-be suitor. In this way he obtained a number of valuable skins.

One night in winter he heard an unusually loud commotion in the barn, so he blocked the hole and went in, to find not one but several male otters competing for the favours of his female. Things got quite hectic as he laid about him with the flail. But when all quietened down he found to his dismay that he had killed his own pet otter as well as the visitors, and with her the goose that laid the golden egg. It is said that he was so upset that he never harmed another otter for as long as he lived.

One cold, dark and blustery evening in late winter a knock came to our door. The man who stood there holding the sack was our Church of Scotland minister. 'It's an otter,' he said, holding out the humping bundle. 'I think it has been run over by a car.' I took the offering gingerly, wondering how on earth I was going to deal with an obviously fairly large injured animal.

We were already in a state of some turmoil as we were in the middle of 'flitting', or moving house. My commitments, particularly office and photographic work, had built up to the stage where our tiny cottage was bursting at the seams. Rather than trying to extend the cottage I had bought a large old house at the other end of the village which had unexpectedly come on the market.

Luckily the porch which housed my office had already been emptied and this could serve as a temporary home for the otter while I assessed the damage and worked out what to do. An old fish box half-filled with

The remains of an otter house, the method of trapping used in times past.

hay would serve as a bed, while a table-top of fine walnut I had salvaged would provide some sort of security propped across the open doorway into the living-room.

What a poor bedraggled and miserable animal emerged from the sack. It was a small female otter, probably not even fully grown, and obviously her back-end had taken the blow because she could only drag herself along by the forepaws. But she still hissed in some sort of defiance as we tried to find out whether any bones were broken.

There wasn't a lot we could do apart from providing food and water, giving the otter some antibiotics and leaving her for the night. Our bedroom was just a partition away, and at first our sleep was interrupted by occasional bursts of the high-pitched whistle that is the otter's main contact call, but later in the night all was quiet.

When I peered in next morning the otter was curled up in the fish box sound asleep, looking much drier and fluffier, and, what was more important, some of the bits of fish we had provided had gone. Perhaps she wasn't as badly hurt as we had feared. Only time would tell.

It is well known that otter cubs, if taken young, can be quite tame and affectionate, although with age they may become destructive and unpredictable. But how would this animal, which was probably about a year old, react to living with humans for a while?

There were two ways of dealing with her. We could either keep her as isolated as possible and merely provide the basic needs while she got better. Or she could stay in the house, in constant human contact and enjoying a limited freedom. Knowing that otters have needle-sharp teeth and are quite prepared to use them if they are startled or frightened, the last option seemed a bit dodgy, but we decided to play it by ear and keep her in the house for the time being.

Well, time and food worked wonders, and at the end of a week the otter was beginning to use all four legs again. Evidently nothing had been seriously damaged in her encounter with the car.

She seemed to accept us warily as benefactors, or at least as providers of the fish fillets which satisfied her hunger. She didn't stay in the porch for long but climbed over the barricade to make herself familiar with every inch of our living-room, which had become her new territory. Otters seem to have a very positive visual memory for familiar objects encountered on their travels. Our otter showed this by immediately recognising anything different, such as a shopping bag or a pair of outdoor boots, and viewing it with great suspicion until she had carefully assessed it by thorough sniffing.

As it was winter, fish supplies were not too easily available, but with the help of the local processing factory we could get enough offcuts of various fish species to feed our guest. While she showed no particular preferences, she did have an aversion to one particular species, the monk or angler fish. Before beginning her meal she would sniff out any bits of monkfish and remove them from the dish. To humans the monkfish is an expensive delicacy, but for some reason our otter wouldn't swallow it.

She knew that the fish supply was kept in the fridge and, if she was hungry, would go into the kitchen and sniff at the fridge door, then watch expectantly for one of us to open it. We tried deliberately to go about our daily work and not to tame the animal, but in less than two weeks she would put her forepaws on my knee, take titbits of fish from my fingers, and curl up to sleep in front of the living-room fire like a dog.

Although she was showing signs of house-training in that she would spraint on a newspaper in one particular corner of the front porch, the smell was beginning to get a little too obvious. So I constructed an enclosure for her up at the new house and transferred her to her new quarters.

It was never our intention to keep her imprisoned, but to return her to the wild as soon as she had recovered. In the event she made the

Opposite *Beautiful, graceful animals, otters seem almost to take on the colour of their surroundings.*

Opposite *Places otters love to play and make their homes. The little stream at Lumbister on Yell.*

Otters frequent the sheltered shores where they find plentiful supplies of the fish on which they feed.

decision herself. One night she climbed over the six-foot fence and was gone. We did not see her again, but the following winter during a snowy spell I found otter tracks leading from the sea up to our house. There the animal had left a small heap of spraints on the doorstep. Was it our otter checking out once-familiar territory? We will never know.

Otters are elusive animals and it took me many years to learn where their breeding places were. The eating places, resting places and the regular paths are all marked in subtle ways by the passing animals, but sometimes hours of waiting are necessary to catch sight of an otter. I often wish I had listened and learned more from 'Shootin' Willie', whose knowledge of the ways of otters would have been the envy of many a modern naturalist.

Just to see the occasional otter didn't really satisfy me, however. Perhaps it was the primitive hunting instinct trying to get out, but I got a great deal of satisfaction in later years when I could afford a camera and telephoto lens. Hunting otters with a camera is every bit as demanding as hunting with a gun. Over the years I have tried many techniques. I built a hide from rocks near an otter holt and stayed in it all night hoping to get a photograph at dawn. When dawn – and the otter – arrived I was so cramped and stiff with cold that I couldn't work the camera properly, and the otter was gone before I could get a picture!

120

'Wait and see' hides built near the shoreline were a bit more productive – but not of otters. Seals, eider ducks and mergansers came swimming past and were photographed. Oystercatchers, gulls and even rock pipits came and perched nearby, but there was never a glimpse of an otter.

Finally I came to the conclusion that the only sensible approach to the problem was simply to walk the shores, keeping as low a profile as possible and trusting that my eyesight was more acute than an otter's. Once an animal is spotted either fishing offshore, eating, grooming or just sleeping on the shore, then all the old skills of stalking are brought into play. Too close an approach can be counter-productive because camera shutters tend to be noisy. It is amazing how at the 'clunk' of a shutter a relaxed, sleepy-looking otter can in an instant be transformed into a brown flash and a string of bubbles. Once an otter has taken fright and decided to do the disappearing trick, no amount of stalking, waiting or searching will ever bring it back.

In Shetland, otters are most often to be seen along low rocky shores, where sub-littoral beds of kelp give shelter to small fish such as butterfish, sea-scorpions and lumpsuckers on which the animals often feed. They also follow streams to the hill lochs where they catch eels and trout. Breeding holts may be well inland. Cracks and holes in the peat are often used, and the parent will travel a mile or more to the sea to catch fish for the growing cubs.

A family of otters on the shore. These young are almost big enough to lead independent lives.

In some parts of their range otters are said to produce cubs at any time throughout the year, but in Shetland I believe they tend to be more seasonal. I have found that they are most active in daytime during the first four months of the year. This is probably when most females come on heat and males worry about territorial rights. During May, June and into July they are much more elusive. The regular spraint heaps, their territory markers, dry up and are no longer maintained. This period is probably when most females are pregnant or have young cubs hidden in the holts.

It is later in the autumn that one has the best chance of seeing a family of otters at play. There is a strong attachment between mother and cubs, and I have often been alerted by hearing the high-pitched squeaking whistle of cubs, worried because mum has been out of touch for a few minutes.

The advent of oil in the seventies was a new experience for otters as well as for other Shetlanders, and they have generally adapted very well. They are active in and around the huge oil terminal at Sullom Voe where 'Beware Otters Crossing' signs have been erected to warn motorists. But they couldn't cope with oil spilled in the sea. Fortunately there has only been one significant oil spill, when the infamous *Esso Bernica* incident occurred soon after the terminal opened for business. Over a thousand tons of oil spilled into the sea and polluted many miles of coastline, killing several thousand sea-birds and at least twenty otters. Most of the animals died after being contaminated with oil on the sea or the beaches, but some appeared to have been poisoned by eating oiled sea-birds.

Surely an unusual picture – five otters together on the shores of Basta Voe.

One or two otter cubs were rescued after their mother had become oiled and presumably died. One of these provided a good example of the dangers of their becoming too familiar with humans. A baby otter had been heard squeaking near the ferry terminal on Yell for a day or two. When Jim Smith heard it he decided to attempt a rescue. The cub was tiny, hungry and forlorn, but when Jim introduced it to his family of children, dogs and cats the little otter needed no further favours. It went out at night with the cats and was scratching at the door for its breakfast in the morning. It learned new skills quickly, finding out for instance that it is unwise to sleep underneath the bonnet of a car when someone is liable to come out and start the engine. It was allowed full freedom to roam, and established a holt down at the freshwater loch nearby, coming to the house only when hungry or to romp with the rest of the family.

But its familiarity was its undoing when it discovered that the neighbour's chickens were tame, stupid and tasted good. People had to barricade their hen-houses to protect their stock and Jim found that human relationships were taking a turn for the worse. We discussed the problem and decided that banishment might be an answer.

By this time the otter was living the good life and not coming home any more, so trapping appeared to be the answer. A box trap set near a hen-house did the trick. The otter was captured and taken by boat to an offshore island, where we hoped it would return to a natural life and forget the taste of chicken.

But it was not to be. Only a week later a crofter at the other end of the island came out to feed his chickens to find an otter blissfully asleep in his hen-house on top of a mattress of chicken feathers. Exit one otter who didn't know the rules and paid the penalty. Ignorance never has been an excuse in the eyes of the law.

Migrants

Lying in front of me as I write are the tattered remains of a book. The covers are missing, pages here and there are torn or scribbled on. It has been pored over, fought over and has suffered the ravages of a family of children. It was my first bird book. Nostalgia floods back as I turn the pages, and I remember the delight I felt when my father gave me Kirkman and Jourdain's *British Birds* as a combined Christmas and birthday present.

Surely, I thought then, I would be able to identify some of the strange birds which, at certain times of the year, appeared as if by magic after a south-easterly gale. Where they came from or where they went was a mystery as yet unsolved by me, but it seemed important that I should at least learn their names.

The fact that I didn't know the English names for many of our local birds was not so important because they all had Shetland names which served our purpose. Nevertheless it was great fun to look up local birds in my new book and find out what they were called in English. There were some surprises. The bird we called a lintie and I had thought would be the English linnet was apparently called twite; I thought this a silly name and continued to think of it as a lintie. The bird we knew as the stinkle or stanechakker was not the stonechat but the wheatear.

Then I learned, almost with horror, that my bird book was not even to be trusted. When off in the bay fishing with my grandfather, we would sometimes see a little group of black and white birds skimming past the boat, alternately flapping and gliding and always holding their wings stiffly extended like a fulmar. 'There's the cockersüdies,' my grandfather would say. 'There'll be fish around.' Try as I might I could not find an illustration in my book which looked like a cockersüdie, and it was ages before I realised it was a Manx shearwater. The artist who depicted the birds flying with wings bent like a stooping peregrine had probably never seen them alive in his life!

But I still loved my bird book despite its limitations. It covered only some of the birds which passed on migration, and when I was really stumped I used to cycle the four miles over to Mid Yell to see Charlie Inkster, who not only knew a great deal about birds but had lots of books which I could browse through. I learned that most of our migrants came from Scandinavia, where the woods were full of breeding

Opposite, above *Every year in spring and autumn migrant birds come to Shetland from Scandinavia. This bluethroat breeds in the woods of Lapland.*

Opposite, below *This migrant waxwing was brought in with a damaged wing. It responded to care and feeding and spent the rest of the winter in my greenhouse.*

Above *Rare birds can turn up at any time. This purple heron from Mediterranean regions was seen by the roadside in Shetland.*

Right *A pectoral sandpiper. This rare wader from America fed in a roadside pool on Yell.*

126

brambling and chaffinch, willow warbler and goldcrest, and the scrub and marshes held bluethroats, blue-headed wagtails and many more.

My job with the RSPB was primarily concerned with the conservation of breeding bird populations, so migrant watching was to me akin to a sport and therefore to be pursued even more assiduously.

At migration times many people head off to the south tip of Shetland. Nearest point to fabulous Fair Isle, it certainly seems to attract a lot of birds, and many rarities have been seen in the bushes, the fields or along the fences. I had known about Fair Isle and its Bird Observatory, but for me it was about as easy to get to as the moon. On starting work for the RSPB, however, I needed a permit to ring birds, and where could I get more expert tuition than from the Warden on Fair Isle?

Shetland can get huge 'falls' of migrants, but they tend to be scattered over a fairly wide area. In Fair Isle the birds are more concentrated and therefore easier to find. On my first visit I added about a dozen new birds to my life list as well as learning to extract birds from traps and mist-nets and to practise the delicate art of clamping numbered alloy rings on the legs of tiny goldcrests and warblers.

Surely red-footed falcons shouldn't be in Shetland? They are a native of the Mediterranean, wintering further south in Africa. A bad case of over-shooting.

I was very aware, when I took on responsibility for all of Shetland, that there were many areas I had never visited. One of these was the little group of islands called Out Skerries. As these islands lie further east than any other point in Shetland and as most of our migrants come from the east, it seemed logical that the islands would prove attractive to the birds – and so they do.

Since I only had a small open boat with a temperamental paraffin engine, the sixteen-mile trip could only be undertaken in quiet weather – not the kind which brings in migrant birds. On my first autumn trip to Skerries I took a tent and camped out, ignoring the warning from an old Skerries lady of a 'size nine' gale. In the middle of the night the wind indeed rose to a real howler and my tent began to disintegrate. All I could do was to wrap what remained round me and go back to sleep.

Next morning, however, the place was knee deep in birds! Flocks of redwing, fieldfare and song thrush were flying about everywhere, harried by a sparrowhawk which had never had it so good. Every potato patch was heaving with warblers. I saw willow warbler, chiffchaff, blackcap, garden warbler, common and lesser whitethroat and many more. From walls and fences pied and spotted flycatchers were hawking insects, as were swallows, house and sand martins along the shoreline. Tired wrynecks were trying to find food along grassy banks, while bluethroats and goldcrests tried to hide in the cabbages. On the stubble, flocks of finches and buntings foraged as tree pipits 'tseeped' overhead. By nightfall I had counted nearly eighty species.

Since then I have visited Out Skerries whenever possible during the spring and autumn migration periods and have seen many rare and exciting birds. Out Skerries is now served by a car ferry and is regularly visited by birdwatchers. These have added many species to the list, which now stands at over 220 – not bad for a few bare acres of island.

The offshore installations can provide a useful resting place for tired migrants. This blackcap was photographed on Ninian Central Oil Platform.

Boats

'A wet sheet and a flowing sea . . .' It almost goes without saying that boats and the sea play an important part in any island community. Shetland is certainly no exception, and it has long been the custom for 'men to toil upon the sea, their women to worry at home'. Although I was not to lead a professional seafaring life, many of my forebears were fishermen, whalers or merchant seamen, and a number of them lost their lives following their calling.

To understand how this way of life evolved we must take a brief look at the past history of Shetland.

When the Norsemen came to raid and plunder, and finally to settle and rule in Shetland before the end of the ninth century, they found that other people had got here first. Picts, Celts, call them what you will, comparatively little is known about their primitive culture, although Shetland has a number of stone artefacts and ruins believed to be from this era. Best known are the brochs. All round the islands, on headlands and prominent places, large heaps of stones, some with sections of masonry still standing, show where these impressive forts once stood. Most have been plundered and the stone used to build houses and walls, but we are fortunate that at least one has stood up to the ravages of time. It is a tribute to the original builders that the great circular broch of Mousa still stands over forty feet tall.

The small island of Mousa lies a mile or so off the east side of the south mainland of Shetland. It is well worth a visit, not only to marvel at the broch, but also to glimpse one of the most elusive sea-birds that nest round our shores. The walls of the broch and the boulder beach nearby house a large colony of storm petrels and, during the short summer night, the island is filled with their bat-like flutterings and soft churring calls.

Leaving these magical birds and returning to Scottish history, we can only guess at how the broch builders were integrated into Viking Shetland. We do know that the islands were probably used as a base, or at least a staging-post, for the Viking raids further south in Britain.

The following period was a more peaceful one. In the year 1469 Shetland was in the possession of King Christian I of Denmark. He was embroiled in a long-standing argument with the King of Scotland about payment for lands formerly owned by the Norsemen and, during the

Overleaf *This traditional type of Shetland seine-netter has now largely been replaced by larger steel boats.*

129

course of their negotiations, it was arranged for his daughter Princess Margaret to marry King James III of Scotland. Her dowry was set at sixty thousand florins, which was more than the Danish king could raise. So the Crown lands of first Orkney and then Shetland were pledged to the Scottish Crown to compensate for the shortfall. This was theoretically a temporary measure, but any attempts to redeem the islands were thwarted and Shetland stayed Scottish until, with the Union of the Crowns, it became part of the United Kingdom of Great Britain.

The period following the Scottish take-over was not the happiest in Shetland history. The Scottish court was plagued by unruly and lawless noblemen, and it is little wonder that they sent the worst of them away to govern the distant earldom of Orkney and Shetland. Thus men like Earl Patrick Stewart came to Shetland, to bully and tyrannise the unwilling islanders. He conscripted people to help build his castle, which can be seen today looming over Scalloway, the ancient capital of Shetland. But Viking blood was still running through the veins of the native population of Shetland, and it was many years before the people reluctantly accepted Scottish rule.

It is only some two hundred years since the old Norse language finally ceased to be the normal speech of Shetlanders. Even now the dialect spoken throughout the islands is a mixture of old Norse, Scots and English, which may sound unintelligible to foreign ears.

Today the desire for independence still at times shows through. There are half-joking remarks about taking up a collection to redeem the pledge made by King Christian and go back to Scandinavian rule – especially when irksome laws with little local relevance are forced upon the islanders by a government far away in London. But through all this the island people have evolved a way of life largely based on crofting and fishing. Self-sufficiency is a way of life rather than an ideal, and isolation has bred a love of an island home which is often fiercely protective.

But, to return to our history, the absence of regular communications meant that development was undoubtedly slow. When steamships were regularly crossing the Atlantic, Shetland men were still rowing forty miles out into the ocean in open boats to fish. Their boats were called 'sixareens', meaning six-oared-ones, and were directly descended from the Norse galleys of old. Evolved to survive in the storm-tossed North Sea, they were graceful, sea-kindly double-ended boats which, properly handled, could survive through dreadful weather. But the best boats and stoutest men sometimes succumbed, and there were many tragedies when sudden severe storms caught a fleet of these open boats many miles offshore. Two of my great-great-grandfathers perished in the storm of July 1832, when over thirty boats were lost. Many were the tales and songs of despair and heroism told of that fateful day. But, in spite of the hardships, a genuine love of the seafaring life was bred into many Shetland men. One of my great-uncles had been thirty-five seasons at the Greenland whaling when a female relative suggested that he was surely too old to go back again. 'I will go as long as I am able to break a ship's biscuit!' he declared. The next season, he was crushed while helping to free the ship from the ice-floes. Though he survived, he never went back to the whaling.

Shetlanders have always had a reputation as seamen. During the Napoleonic Wars, ships would be sent up to the islands to recruit extra men for the fleet. Recruitment was pretty basic and consisted of rounding up suitable candidates and pressing them into service. Every trick in the book was used to escape the press-gang but, once they were subdued, Shetlanders often rose to positions of command, acquitting themselves well at battles such as Trafalgar.

The first boat I was allowed to set foot in as a boy was a 'fourareen' or 'whilly', a small rowing boat similar in shape to the larger 'sixareen' but arranged for four men to row. The pedigree of these boats is unquestionably Scandinavian. Now designed and built in Shetland, in former days they were set up in Norwegian boatyards, dismantled, and sent across as do-it-yourself kits to be reassembled in the islands. Longer, slimmer versions, called 'yoals', can still be seen in the south Mainland of Shetland and in Fair Isle. Although the shape was said to have evolved to enable the boats to cope with the short steep seas and tidal overfalls of that area, they are also extremely fast under oars. This was vital for intercepting passing sailing boats so that island produce could be bartered for goods or luxuries unobtainable locally.

Nowadays many small boats are made of fibreglass, but in my youth all were wooden planked and painted or tarred annually. The smell of fir tar on the inside of a boat, heated by the sun, is one of the most evocative scents I know.

The beach at Aywick was, and still is, too exposed to allow boats to lie safely at a mooring, so they had to be small enough to be pulled up the beach. This precluded the use of an inboard engine, and when I was a boy outboards were hardly on the market. So it was a case of either oars or sail. As most of our fishing grounds were within a mile or two of the village, we nearly always rowed. No commercial fishing was carried on from Aywick in my lifetime, but neither were there fish shops or travelling fish vans. Every household having able-bodied men – or boys – was assured of a plentiful supply of fresh fish during the summer, and any surplus was salted down in barrels or salted and sun-dried for winter use. Households which had no one able to go fishing were not forgotten. It was all part of the ritual, especially for the youngsters, to take strings of fish round to the neighbours, where they were usually rewarded with a sweetie or other titbit.

Opportunistic fishing was usually done by dangling baited hand-lines over the boat, positioned over an area which was known from past

*The graceful shapes of
Fair Isle 'yoals' pulled up
out of reach of the sea.*

experience to attract certain kinds of fish. The boat was set in place by using cross-bearing or 'meids', lining up landmarks such as a house or prominent rock with a feature on the skyline. In this manner a boat could be stationed very accurately over a reef or a patch of sand invisible to the eye thirty fathoms below.

A story was told of a certain man whose eyesight was not very good and who, by luck rather than judgement, came on a fine shoal of fish. As was the practice, he immediately scanned the shoreline to 'take a meid'. A prominent white mark was chosen, bearing above a certain rock but, when he went out next day to relocate the fish, there was no white mark to be seen. He had used a white cow as a mark, and she had moved on!

I have spent many blissful hours drifting gently with the currents, trying to tempt the fat grey and white haddocks to take the bait into their large, soft-lipped mouths before it was snatched by a sharp-toothed whiting or an unwanted dogfish. Sometimes a plague of these miniature sharks would invade the fishing grounds, causing us to abandon our task until they went away. Certain kinds of fish were taboo in our area for no apparent reason. No one would have considered eating eels or dogfish, although elsewhere they may be considered delicacies.

We did, however, have a use for the tail and fins of the piked dogfish. These were cut off and collected until there were enough to make into a small parcel, which was wrapped in rough hessian, tied up securely with string and placed in a sea-water pool. Anchored down with a few rocks, the parcel of fins and tails would be left for thirty days, after which it would be recovered. By this time all traces of flesh would have rotted away, leaving only the fine cartilaginous filaments which all the shark family have instead of bones. These filaments were shiny and translucent, and when a small bunch of them was tied on as 'busk' or dressing to a hook, it made an attractive lure for saithe or pollack.

Small boys were tolerated well enough at the inshore fishing. We could be tucked away in the bows of the boat and given our own hand-line to dangle. But the more serious business of going further out to set the long-lines was a different matter. This was man's work, and there was little room in a small boat for anyone other than three or four men, their creels of lines and – if all had gone well – a big cargo of fish on the way back.

A long-line consisted of up to six 'buchts' of line, each bucht being sixty fathoms (120 yards), with hooks on short snoods fastened every six feet or so. Each of the crew had at least one haddock-line already baited and coiled up in a wooden creel, plus buoys and buoy-ropes, 'kappies' and 'bighters' – shaped stones used as anchors for the line – so that when all this was shot there could be over 3000 baited hooks covering three miles of sea-bed.

An appropriate end for an old boat no longer fit for the sea, turned upside down and used as a roof for a sheep-house.

Gutting fish at dawn on the fishing boat Halcyon *near Out Skerries. The gulls get a considerable amount of their winter food from attending the fishing boats.*

The type of bait used was governed by what was available. Shellfish such as cockles or mussels were ideal but not easily come by on exposed coasts such as those around Aywick, and we often had to resort to the less desirable limpets. These would be collected the day before by the simple expedient of knocking them off the rocks exposed at low tide, using an old wood chisel as a limpet-pick. They were put in a pan of water on the fire to be 'leepit', brought to the stage where the shells could be easily removed, this process being known as 'shilling'.

Sometimes limpets were alternated with small pieces of salted mackerel; the baited hooks were then laid in rows, separated by strips of newspaper to prevent them becoming tangled when they were shot over the side of the boat.

Apart from the highly desired haddock, many other types of fish would be tempted to take the bait. Flatfish and skate were acceptable, while spiky gurnard, although perfectly edible, were often discarded as not worth the effort of skinning. Beautiful iridescent dragonets would be removed carefully and thrown back, in the knowledge that their spines were mildly poisonous and that the wound, like that made by the spike of the 'hoe' or dogfish, would certainly fester and be very painful. Small squid and octopus were usually shaken off before they came in over the gunwale, lest they squirt their ink and spoil the fish already caught. But sometimes, as a prank, a small octopus would be placed on an unsuspecting crew-member's shoulder. An exploring tentacle in the ear was guaranteed to get a good response!

One day, when the wind was blowing offshore, I had drifted further out than I intended. I was having a stiff pull against the breeze and my arms were beginning to tire a bit when round the headland came a sight which nearly made me drop my oars. It was a little fourareen, not much bigger than the one I was rowing, but it was belting along at five or six knots with a bow-wave and a wash creaming behind. As it came nearer I recognised Bob from over the hill, sitting at the tiller with his pipe between his teeth and a broad smile on his face. 'Like a tow?' he called, and I thankfully flung over the end of my painter. Sitting there in my boat, with the water rushing by and my aching arms folded, I was in heaven. I resolved that one day I too would have a boat like Bob Mouat's. Many years were to pass before that dream came true, and it was only after I got married and moved from Aywick to live beside the sheltered water of Mid Yell Voe that I began to think seriously of getting a boat of my own.

In the meantime I never let slip an opportunity to go boating or fishing. I sailed with my brother-in-law in local regattas, took part in outboard motor races with borrowed boats – on one occasion losing my boss's new Seagull outboard when the stern of the boat fell off and took the motor with it to the bottom of the sea. I tried commercial fishing on a seine-net boat for a short spell and found out, among other things, that I wasn't entirely immune to sea-sickness when the going got really rough. I also found out what a tough life that of a real fisherman can be: fishing through the night, gutting and cleaning by day until you were too tired and sleepy to hold the slippery fish or the gutting knife, and then setting out on the long haul to the market in Aberdeen in the teeth of a south-easterly gale. Had there been a permanent berth for me I might have stayed with the *Halcyon*, but I was only on board as a relief for a sick crew member, and fate led me in a different direction.

Opposite above *Manx shearwater breed in small numbers on Fetlar and Yell and are often seen in the evenings a little distance offshore.*

Opposite below *A popular and well-loved bird in Shetland is the oyster-catcher. A summer visitor, it arrives in Shetland about March and departs again in late summer after having reared a family.*

Below *Even winter boat trips can be quite exciting. I disturbed this King Eider in Sullom Voe.*

Still hankering after a boat of my own, I bought and converted a 'Shetland model', originally built as a sailing racer. I put in decks and a little wheel shelter, and installed a 7 horsepower Swedish engine which ran smoothly on paraffin and carried *Roselyn* and me many safe and happy miles.

It was about this time that I embarked on the career which was to take me through more than two decades of my working life – a career which justified my continuing to do those things I had looked on as hobbies, boating, photography and birdwatching. Before long *Roselyn* had to go. She could no longer cope with the demands put on her and when, one night, on the way back from a storm petrel ringing session on Fetlar, I split one of her boards just by punching into a head sea, I knew the time had come to start looking around for something bigger.

I found what I was looking for not far away; she was a 28-foot 'fyvie', built in 1948 for the tough task of fishing the North Sea from her home port of Peterhead. Her sweet lines were not enhanced by a 'square box' wheelhouse, but I knew that *Consort* had the potential to take me safely through whatever my courage – or lack of it – demanded of her.

And so it proved to be. In twenty years she never once gave me cause for concern. Any mishaps have been entirely of my own making and, where my inexperience or plain foolishness got us into danger, her centuries-old pedigree and sea-kindly character got us out of it.

139

Photography

I had developed an interest in photography as a young boy just before the war. Simple box cameras were not uncommon then, and my father had a slightly more sophisticated Kodak VP (I thought it meant vest pocket) folding camera which had a means of setting various distances and a tiny right-angle viewfinder. Colour films were rare. Usually the camera only came out to take snaps of aunts and uncles and other more distant relatives who came to visit, always associated in my mind with the smell of camphor and mothballs. But if I saved up for a spool of film I was allowed to experiment, and naturally my first aim was to photograph a bird of some kind.

Knowing nothing of telephoto lenses, hides or any of the paraphernalia used by bird photographers, I had to work out for myself some method of getting close to my quarry, and obviously some sort of concealment was necessary. Sparrows, starlings and twite were common round the crofts, especially in the stackyards, and these were my first subjects. I hid inside a conveniently empty water butt and tried to take pictures through the bung hole. I didn't fully appreciate that the viewfinder was not on the same plane as the lens of the camera – the word 'parallax' was not yet in my vocabulary – so the results were pretty dismal, consisting mostly of out-of-focus snaps of the inside of a water barrel.

Only slightly more successful were attempts to outwit the curlew which came in from the hills after the hay was cut, to probe with their long beaks for grubs and insects among the shorn grass. The partly dried hay was piled up in little haycocks we call 'coles' and these offered concealment. Unfortunately my preparations scared off the flock of curlew, but I was convinced that they would soon return after I had burrowed deep inside the cole, leaving only a small aperture through which to take photographs.

I knew how important it was to remain still and quiet, and the first half-hour or so was not too bad. Then the itching started. I was wearing short trousers and could feel various small tickling movements on my bare legs. My imagination ran riot. I had been reading at school about scorpions and tarantulas and in my mind's eye I could see similarly horrible insects poised to sink their lethal fangs into my unprotected backside! I was beginning to sweat and squirm when I was discovered by our Shetland collie, who was convinced I was playing games specially for her benefit. In spite of whispered entreaties to go away and leave me alone she insisted on burrowing into the hay as well. Eventually she grew tired of my lack of response and went off to look for a more co-operative playmate, leaving me to my vigil.

Nothing happened for ages and I think I must have dozed off. But I was instantly awake when I heard the calls of the returning curlew as they landed at the far side of the field. And there they stayed. For half an hour or more they pecked and probed well out of range. Whether they could sense my presence or had merely found a good feeding patch I never knew, but eventually they all took off down to the shore to continue feeding on the ebbing tide. I did take a token photograph, but in the tiny square prints that came back from the shop I couldn't find the curlew even with a magnifying glass.

Tactics like these were obviously not much good. I almost gave up the idea of bird photography, realising that my father's precious camera was just not right for the job. Then I remembered the fulmar. In those days fulmar petrels were not nearly as widespread and familiar as they are today, and most nests were situated on grassy ledges on steep, if not necessarily very high, cliffs. On one of my secret jaunts in the cliffs of Ramnageo I had climbed on to a ledge where I had been challenged by a sitting fulmar, or mally as we call them. Instead of leaving her large white egg and flying off, she opened her beak in threat posture and I, with due regard to the narrowness of the ledge and the unpleasant and incriminating effects of fulmar oil, had found an alternative path. Surely this was a suitable subject for the camera.

I watched for my chance and, when the next opportunity came to slip away, I went back to Ramnageo complete with camera and a new spool of film. It was no surprise to find the fulmar still sitting on her egg because their incubation period is between seven and eight weeks. As I was also aware that they are very reluctant to leave the nest, even at the approach of a human, it promised to be a fairly simple matter of climbing down to the level of the bird, then worming my way nearer and nearer until I was within shooting distance. Having looked at similar sized rocks through the viewfinder, I judged that I would need to be about three feet away before the bird appeared big enough to get a good photograph.

Everything went as planned, and when I got within a couple of yards I lay down on my stomach and, pushing the camera in front, edged nearer and nearer. Even the tiny click of the shutter sounded loud in my ears, but still the bird sat and I squirmed forward another foot. 'Click' . . . and I had taken my first real bird photograph. I had also never been so close to a wild bird before, and from a distance of less than three feet I admired the fulmar's soft white plumage, the dark inscrutable eye and strangely lined beak.

Overleaf *Winter can have its tranquil moments. A party of cormorants on a shingle bar at Sullom Voe.*

141

A fulmar on her nest – my first real photograph of a bird. My father did a drawing on the back of the photograph showing the lengths to which he thought I had gone to get this view.

I should have been warned when the fulmar's white breast began to heave, but in my euphoric state I was quite unprepared for the stomachful of foul-smelling oil which splattered all over my head and the camera. Fulmar oil is an incredibly persistent substance and, short of running away to sea, I knew I was going to have to go home and take the consequences. Of course it resulted in my being banned yet again from the cliffs, but the thrill of looking at those first photographs stayed with me for many a day – although the camera was never quite the same afterwards.

During the war we were forbidden to carry binoculars, far less cameras, and anyway film was unobtainable. So any thoughts of photography as a hobby were put aside for a number of years. After the war my pittance of a wage as an apprentice baker did not allow for expensive hobbies like photography.

In 1951 I was called up for National Service. Looking on it as an ideal chance to see something of the world, I immediately put my name in for overseas service. The fact that the Korean war was going strong at the time didn't dampen my enthusiasm, and the only time I chickened out was when, having been posted to Korea, I couldn't pluck up the courage to tell my parents. Instead, I told them I was going to Hong Kong. In the event I didn't have to tell any more fibs because, while on a troopship somewhere in the China Sea, I learned that I had been re-posted to No 1 Bakery, Kowloon.

The urge to take hundreds of photographs was strong, but money was very scarce. Promotion to sergeant meant extra pay, and my chance came when a mate, desperately trying to raise some cash, sold me a pawn ticket which he said could be exchanged for an excellent German camera. It was a Solida 111, now a long-forgotten marque, which used roll film and had a Schneider lens that pulled out and twisted into place like the early Leica. Being stuck in the city and its environs for much of the time, I didn't find much in the natural history line to photograph. Even the sea was disappointing, and although I spent a lot of time on – and in – the warm waters, there wasn't even a fulmar to be seen!

Back home, the boring business of making a living took precedence. But after a few years the urge to photograph birds and animals asserted itself again. The photographic press was by then announcing the birth of a new era in photography, that of the Single Lens Reflex camera with its choice of lenses, viewing systems and all the other advantages which really brought system photography within reach of most interested amateurs.

Initially the choice was still limited, and the better makes were prohibitively expensive, but among the 'bargain buys' to come on the market was the Praktica, made in East Germany and subsidised by the state. So, for the sum of £28.10s I became the owner of a Praktica FX3 and embarked on the compulsive hobby of buying, selling, losing, swopping, coveting and amassing camera equipment. This goes on to the present day, as new and tempting bits of necessary and expensive equipment come on the market.

An anxious dunlin contrasting nicely with a lady's-smock near a peaty pool on Fetlar.

In 1964 my job with the RSPB opened up many exciting possibilities and challenges. I now had a good reason for continuing my rather expensive hobby of photography, and before long I was using my growing collection of slides of birds and other wildlife to illustrate talks about Shetland. My first slide show was to a local Women's Institute, and it turned out to be quite an eventful evening.

There was no mains electricity in the hall, the main lighting being supplied by Tilley paraffin lamps which were dimmed by the simple expedient of letting most of the air out, so I had to borrow a 12-volt projector and a car battery to provide the illumination. I spent days selecting slides and preparing my talk. The projector was so primitive that slides had to be fed in one at a time from a storage box in which they had been placed in sequence. On the night, the President gave a short welcoming speech and I was ready. But when I opened the box, out fell the slides, all over the table and on to the floor, completely wrecking the carefully prepared sequence I had sweated over for days. The explanation was simple. I had opened the box upside down!

I stalked these two otters on the shore at Fetlar. Hand-holding a 400mm lens, I had only a few seconds to compose and take the picture before the otters leapt into the sea.

Then there was the evening in a Scottish university when the hired projector got stuck on 'automatic' and started rattling through slides at a rate of one every three seconds. I kept up bravely for a time, talking at speed like an auctioneer at a cattle market, and was bathed in perspiration when someone found a switch and stopped the machine at about slide sixteen. There were profuse apologies from the chairman, and then the projectionist signalled that he had solved the problem. We were off again, but this time he had found the 'reverse' switch. The machine fairly belted through the slides – all the way back to the beginning. The chairman was apoplectic, and the audience was in stitches. But it came right in the end.

Of course problems are not all due to mechanical equipment going wrong. Human error can play its part and so can acts of God. The slide show season is during the winter months, and especially up here in the islands weather plays a large part. Snow, icy roads and gales can all contribute to cancellations, but one evening I encountered another weather problem. The hall in which I was to give my slide show, like many of the older buildings in Shetland, was roofed with corrugated iron sheets without any sort of insulation. Shortly after I started my slide show a violent hail storm began and the sound of it on the iron roof was tremendous. Having tried to shout above it to no avail, I had to stop the show until the storm passed over and people could once again hear what was being said.

It was obvious that there was a great deal to learn about photography, and one or two people helped enormously with my education. The first was Dr Ian Brooker, who had been appointed general practitioner for Yell and Fetlar shortly before I began working for the RSPB. Ian and I soon became acquainted, and realised that we had a number of interests in common.

Before coming to Shetland Ian had taken part in an expedition to the Antarctic island of South Georgia in the composite role of medic, naturalist and photographer, and his many exciting adventures included being the first to climb the mountain which now bears the name of Mount Brooker in his honour.

It was Ian who initiated me into the mysteries of darkroom work, and whose equipment I used until such time as I could afford to convert a cupboard under the stairs into a tiny darkroom of my own.

I well remember the thrill of seeing my first bird picture published. I had put up a hide near a lapwing's nest in the field not far from our house, and over the course of a week had moved it up to a position from which I could take a photograph. But when I woke the next morning it was to find a snow-covered landscape. Surely my lapwing would have lost her eggs. But when I went to look from a safe distance, there she was, still sitting on her nest with only her head and tail showing above the snow. By midday the sun was out and the snow was melting fast, so I sneaked into the hide and took some photographs of what to me was a unique event – a bird sitting on her nest in three inches of snow!

Lapwings are among the first birds of the year to nest in Shetland, but this one got caught out by a late snowfall. The snow melted quickly and the bird went on to hatch successfully.

Photographing sea-birds is not always difficult. I could not get closer to this shag without getting my feet wet.

Whenever I see a colony of grey seals I am reminded of the day Ian Brooker and I nearly got stuck in a sea cave while photographing the seals on Fetlar. One of the best breeding colonies of grey seals is in a sort of open cave called Birrier's Geo. This is impossible to climb down to because of overhangs, while pounding breakers make it very hazardous to land there from a boat. However, with our cameras stowed away in protective waterproof bags we scrambled ashore, pulling the dinghy well out of reach of the sea and leaving the motor-boat anchored offshore.

Although we had kept our approach as unobtrusive as possible, we did cause some panic. A group of unattached bulls and cows charged down the beach into the sea, whereupon several of the 'beachmasters', the huge bulls who regard themselves as undisputed leaders, thinking they were being challenged, flung themselves into a snarling attack. Pitched battles ensued in the surf before the younger bulls, who hadn't wanted to fight anyway, escaped out to sea. All over the beach sprawled little bundles of yellowish fur that were the pups. Some were sound asleep, others were gazing around with their great liquid eyes. Many had been suckling when, at our approach, their mothers had rushed off into the sea, leaving them crying and moaning almost like human babies. 'Sounds like a maternity annexe,' commented Ian as we set up our cameras. By no means all the adult seals had left the beach. A number of females stayed with their pups, quite prepared to do battle if we approached too closely.

As we worked happily photographing seal pups and adults from all angles we failed to notice that much heavier seas were breaking on the beach, cutting off our only escape route. We packed up our cameras and waited, hoping that the waves would subside, but if anything they were getting bigger. We worked out a possible plan of action. The dinghy was only about eight feet in length and unlikely to get two of us plus our camera gear safely off the beach. But one of us might make it and could then from the safety of the motor-boat let the empty dinghy ashore on the long line, using it to pull the other person off the beach in the little boat.

I volunteered to make the first attempt. I sat in the dinghy with the oars at the ready, while Ian stood by to push when there was a lull in the seas. 'Now!' he shouted and I started rowing as hard as I could, with Ian shoving until the water was too deep. For a few moments I thought I was going to make it, then I was rowing up a watery hill which got steeper and steeper until with a crash it seemed the world fell on top of me. Instinctively I gulped my lungs full of air as I went under, but I was desperately in need of a fresh supply before the following wave dumped me unceremoniously at Ian's feet. 'Ah, you're back,' he said.

The next attempt was successful, however, and the rest of the plan went smoothly. Soon we were chugging back to Mid Yell as fast as the 'seven horses' could take us. In warm waters the incident would have been fun, but this was Shetland in November, and the sea temperature must have been less than 5°C. We were feeling distinctly chilly by the time we had covered the eight miles back to Mid Yell.

Another person from whom I learned a great deal is Dennis Coutts, a professional photographer working from Lerwick who also has a passion for birds. We hit it off from our first meeting, and I have to admit that I probably got more from the relationship than he did, especially in the early days, for besides his knowledge of photography, Dennis had something I didn't have – a car.

Unlike today, when a system of small car ferries connects all the main inhabited islands of Shetland, in the sixties ferries were generally limited to one or two a day, and were for foot passengers only. If the tides permitted, however, ferry skippers could usually be persuaded to take a small motor-bike on board, where it would be lashed to the rails and usually get a washing with salt water while crossing the tide rips. This was the only means of transport of use to me and, as I had been a keen motor-cyclist since before I was legally entitled to be, the RSPB supplied me with a bike. I was proud of my brand new 250cc AJS, which was the envy of many friends. Few of us had even seen a new motor-bike, far less owned one!

But except in the best of weather, biking is a cold, unsociable means of travel, especially if your normal gear includes camera and binoculars. So I was only too glad to leave the bike behind and join Dennis on weekend trips in his Dormobile. We had some memorable trips, especially at bird migration times. We watched ospreys catching trout in the lochs of Walls and scoured the gardens and crops of Dunrossness for bluethroats, red-breasted flycatchers and hosts of other rare migrants. More than once we came within a whisker of the 'ton', that is a hundred species in a day – quite something in a place like Shetland with its absence of woodlands.

When a male snowy owl took up residence on the island of Whalsay in 1963 we went to try to get some pictures. We were met by our late friend Johnny Simpson, who probably had the keenest eyesight of anyone I have met, and he took us up to the area where the owl had last been seen. For ages we stalked the bird, but it wouldn't co-operate, until in desperation I disguised Dennis as a stack of peats! I dismantled someone's heap of drying peat and rebuilt it around the crouching Dennis. I then went off and gently chivvied the snowy owl in his direction. The owl settled on an adjoining peat-stack just long enough for Dennis to fire off a couple of quick shots before its keen eyes spotted the phoney and it was off. Dennis was so cramped that he couldn't stand, but his picture was the first taken of a snowy owl in Shetland.

Another opportunity for photographing a snowy owl arose during a wedding in Fetlar. Dennis was taking pictures of the bride arriving at the church when the snowy owl flew past. It was terrible to witness his agonies of indecision, but he resisted the impulse to rush off after the owl until he had finished the job he was there to do.

Later that day, as we were discussing with some Fetlar men how we might pursue the owl, one of them suggested jokingly that there was an old pantomime horse costume in a cupboard in the hall. Dennis's face lit up as he turned to me. 'Oh no,' I said, forestalling him. 'I'm not going to be the back end of the horse.' Never one to miss a chance, Dennis rooted out the old moth-eaten costume of wickerwork head and hessian body, and we set out for the hill early next morning. The Nature Conservancy officer, Lance Tickell, was staying in Fetlar and Dennis persuaded him to come along to fasten us into the horse costume.

From nearly a mile away we spotted the owl up on the slope of Vord Hill, so we went round the other side to get 'dressed'. Thank goodness there was nobody around to watch the performance of the ridiculous horse staggering along the hillside with a telephoto lens sticking out of its mouth! At the sight of this apparition, the snowy owl hurriedly departed. Even the oystercatchers weren't fooled but took flight and yelped off into the distance. Stumbling about on a rock-strewn hillside, getting hotter and more claustrophobic by the minute, I was not enjoying myself. The final straw came when the forepart of the horse

reported that a group of Shetland ponies seemed to be taking an interest . . . I sat down on the nearest rock and refused to budge.

Amazingly, the snowy owl stayed around on Fetlar, found a mate the following year and settled down to breed. But I doubt if it ever again saw anything so bizarre in the Fetlar hills.

Many of the old school of photographers – those who considered anything less than a 5 × 4 inch plate camera a toy – have visited Shetland, mainly to photograph the divers, whimbrel, skuas and phalaropes. I was privileged to meet such people as G. K. Yeates, Colonel Niall Rankin, I.M. Thompson and others who not only came to Shetland but wrote books about their experiences. That doyen of bird photographers Eric Hosking visited Shetland for the first time only in 1967 to take pictures of the snowy owls on Fetlar. To this day I have a souvenir of that visit in the Novoflex 400mm lens which I bought from Eric and which is still my favourite for birds in flight or other action shots.

It was Izaak Walton who said 'There is more to fishing than just to fish,' and so it is with photography. Like the whole study of natural history, it can mean anything you want it to – a casual hobby, an absorbing pastime or a lifetime's occupation.

Feeling as foolish as I looked – watching Dennis Coutts get dressed in a pantomime-horse skin to photograph the snowy owl.

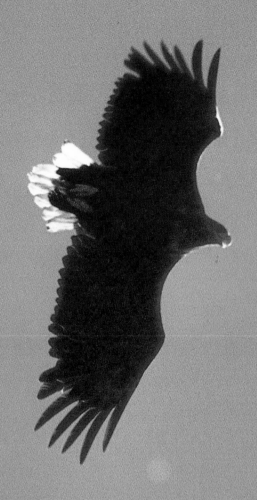

Epilogue
The Sea Eagle and the Baby

Our old school stood in a fairly isolated position, the only other inhabited building within half a mile being the Old Schoolhouse nearby, which was occupied by an old lady called Annie Matthewson. Living near the school meant that she was occasionally subject to pranks played by the more mischievous element. Invariably – but not always justly – blame was laid on the boys, but as the mischief was usually of a minor nature, relationships were fairly peaceable.

Annie's house-companion was a fat old Shetland collie she called 'Shaila', who, though prone to yapping, had no aggressive qualities. This could not be said of Annie's moorit ram. Moorit denotes the rich brown colour of the wool characteristic of some of the Shetland breed of sheep. This animal had a magnificent set of curly horns which it knew how to use to good effect. At playtime the children used to feed the ram with bits of bread, making sure they were on the other side of the playground fence. But it happened from time to time that someone left the gate open, and there the trouble would start.

I suspect this animal had been brought up as a bottle-fed pet, because it feared neither dog nor man, far less a woman teacher and a bunch of kids. I vividly recall one afternoon when the classroom was quiet and peaceful: the only sounds were the occasional squeak of a slate pencil or the shuffle of feet, and our teacher was sitting behind her pedestal desk reading. Suddenly there was a bang. The door swung open and in marched the moorit ram. Now I don't doubt that all the animal wanted was a bit of bread to eat, but the teacher wasn't having any of it. 'Get out!' she shouted. 'Shoo, shoo.' The ram took one look at her waving arms and didn't like what it saw. Down went its head . . . crash! The front of the desk took the first blow and the wood splintered. Crash! The desk toppled over, teacher and all. The class was in pandemonium. The smaller children were screaming and yelling and climbing on to desks, while many of the older pupils were convulsed with laughter. Peace was restored when a few of the older boys grabbed the ram by the horns and steered it out of the door and back to its own domain. This happened shortly after Annie had complained that some of the boys had been up to mischief, and I am sure there was a glint of satisfaction in the old lady's eye when she was told how her ram had invaded the school classroom.

Opposite *Photographed in Iceland, this white-tailed sea eagle is the same species as the bird said to have carried the baby Mary Anderson from Unst to Fetlar.*

155

We often ran messages for old Annie, or helped her on the croft, and when she was in good humour she would reward us with a small spoon of sugar, or tell us stories. One of her stories fascinated me. It concerned a close encounter with a pair of eagles up on the hill beyond the croft.

The white-tailed sea eagle or erne lived in the more remote parts of north and west Britain until shortly after the turn of the century, when as a result of man's persecution it became extinct. The eyries were usually built in inaccessible places on the sea-cliffs, often on a bold headland from which the birds could see for many miles. Their young were mainly fed on fish or carrion which the parents scrounged along the shores. But they were also accused of more serious offences such as killing and carrying off young lambs – and even young babies.

Ernes were quite numerous in Shetland at one time, but by the time Annie Matthewson was a young girl there were probably only about half a dozen pairs left. The last pair to nest had their eyrie at the Neeps of Graveland on the west side of Yell, which was only six miles or so from the croft on which Annie lived.

She told us how, as a girl, she had been sent up into the hills beyond the croft to look for a lost sheep, and finally found the poor thing dead in a bog, with two huge eagles ripping and tearing at the carcass. She described how the startled birds took flight, their huge wings beating the heather as they tried to get airborne. As she watched them fly away over the moor, she had seen a quill come loose from one of the great wings and slowly spiral back to earth. At this point in her story Annie would reach up to a shelf above the fire and take down a roll of faded newspaper tied with a bit of wool. Carefully unwrapping the paper she would bring out a foot-long primary feather with a shaft as thick as a pencil. 'And that', she would say, 'is the feather which I have kept to this day.'

Annie also told us how a baby had been rescued from an erne's nest unharmed, after being carried from Unst to Fetlar. She would add in a matter of fact way that 'some of us are descended from that same bairn.'

Many years later, Charlie Inkster told me that when he was a boy he could remember watching eagles soaring in the sky and 'yelping like dogs'. He also knew the story of the eagle and the baby, but it was not until I talked with the late Jamesie Laurenson of Fetlar that I got at the details.

Jamesie was a noted local historian, a great character and a man of such physical strength that he was truly a legend in his lifetime. One spring day I was over in Fetlar and found Jamesie working at his boat. Securely fastened down in her winter 'noost' she showed signs of long usage with her line-grooved gunwale and evident repairs. 'She was a good boat,' said Jamesie, 'but I doubt if she will last another season.' As he talked it was difficult to believe that this tall, powerful man would soon be celebrating his eightieth birthday.

'Yes,' he said in answer to my question, 'I can certainly tell you the story about the eagle and the baby, and what's more, I can tell it to you exactly as it was told to me by Willa-May Brown, the greatest historian who ever lived in Fetlar.' He laid aside his tar-brush and we wandered over to his house where we settled down by the fire, while his sister put on the kettle and Jamesie began his story.

'It happened in the year 1690, the year they rebuilt the Established church in Fetlar. A man called William Anderson lived with his wife and infant daughter Mary in the croft of Braehead at Norwick in Unst.

'One day in late summer they were out in the field near the house cutting bere [a type of barley] and, as was the custom, they had taken their baby daughter with them. She was wrapped in a warm shawl, sleeping peacefully and tucked in the lee of a stook of sheaves where they could keep an eye on her.

'The ground slopes steeply down towards the sea below the croft, and although an onshore breeze was blowing, it was warm and thirsty work. William's wife suggested they could do with a cup of tea so, laying aside her sickle and checking that the baby was still sleeping, she went off to the cottage to put on the kettle.

'After she had gone, William went up to the end of the field to set up some of the sheaves and was busy at the task when he was alerted either by a sound or a movement. He looked round and was horrified to see an eagle labouring off into the wind, a shawl-clad bundle in its talons.

Photographed a number of years ago, the late Jamesie Laurenson of Fetlar and his brother Gibbie mowing rye-grass. It was Jamesie who told me the details of the story of the eagle and the baby.

157

'He shouted and ran and a neighbour who had heard him also joined in the chase, but the erne gradually gained height and headed off in a southerly direction, still with the tiny figure of his baby daughter in its talons. The men ran until they were exhausted. Other neighbours were alerted and took up the chase, keeping the bird in sight. When they reached the coast the eagle had disappeared out over the sea in the direction of Fetlar, some three miles distant. There, at a place called Bustapund, near the Blue Banks, eagles had had their eyrie since time immemorial.

'At Ramnageo, the point nearest Fetlar, the runners found that all the good boats were out fishing, leaving only an old, leaking boat on the beach. But the situation was desperate, and, taking an extra man to bale, they launched the boat and made speed towards Fetlar.

'Arriving at Fetlar below the croft of Colbinstoft, they explained their mission to the people there, and were told that the eagle's eyrie was under an overhang in an inaccessible part of the cliffs.

'An attempt had to be made, however, and quickly. Ropes were the answer, but again there were problems. With all the boats away the only ropes available were some highly suspect discarded halyards. The best bits were knotted together and the party set out with all haste along the clifftop to the spot above the eagle's nest.

'The would-be rescuers couldn't see directly into the nest but they could just see part of the baby's shawl, so at least this was the right place. Serious doubts were expressed about the ability of the old ropes to support the weight of a man, but a young Fetlar lad called Robert Nicholson, who had joined in to see the fun, immediately volunteered. There was some argument about whether a young boy should be entrusted with such an important task, but he was a wiry chap, well used to cliff climbing, and so he was tied to the rope and lowered over the edge.

'Now then . . .' Jamesie paused. 'There is a slight difference in the story here. One old person told me that tar was rubbed on Robert's soles so that he could get a better grip on the smooth rock, but other historians deny that. Anyway, the boy was carefully lowered down and when he got to the eyrie he saw an amazing sight, one which he often told during his lifetime. There was the baby Mary fast asleep in the eagle's nest with a well-grown young eagle crouched at each side. One even had its beak caught up in the baby's shawl. Robert carefully disentangled the shawl and, with the precious bundle safely in his arms, was hauled back up to the clifftop.

'It was said that amid the congratulations from the helpers, the elderly man taken on to bale the boat, who had by then caught up with the rest, said, "Well done boy, you'll maybe get her for your wife yet!"

'Mary was taken quickly to the croft at Colbinstoft where a nursing mother fed her while preparations were made for the trip back to Unst.

'The amazing thing was that there wasn't a scratch on the baby. The thick shawl had protected her from the talons of the eagle. When the boat reached Unst once more, they were met by the baby's mother, weeping tears of joy at the safe return of her infant.

'Now then,' Jamesie went on, 'we come to an interesting part.

'There is no suitable kind of stone in Fetlar for the manufacture of millstones and, as they were essential household equipment in those days, they had to be imported from the neighbouring islands of Unst and Yell.

'There came a time some years later when a party of Fetlar men were preparing to take a boat across to Unst to collect a consignment of millstones. When Robert Nicholson's mother learned about the trip she encouraged him to go along, saying "Here's a chance for you to go and see the lass you rescued." When they reached Unst, Robert was directed to the croft of Braehead where he made himself known. He was greeted with delight by the family, including Mary who by this time had grown into a pretty young girl.

'It was a case of love at first sight, although,' said Jamesie with a chuckle, 'in his case it was second sight! Eventually the two were married, and came to live in Fetlar.'

Jamesie paused for a moment's thought. 'Now we come to the ancestry. Mary Anderson, who was rescued, was the great-grand-mother of James Andrew Jamieson, who lived at Houbie in Fetlar. He had a daughter who married a man called Petrie . . .' He went on to list all the people still living in Fetlar, including my own relatives, who were directly descended from Mary Anderson. Each step of the ancestry was stressed by a tap on the table from a great gnarled forefinger, still smeared with tar from the boat. Any thoughts of arguing with the plausibility of the tale evaporated as he transferred the tapping to my knee and said with a steely glint in his eye, 'Don't let anyone tell you the story is a fable – for I know it to be true.'

Saxby in his *Birds of Shetland* (1874) offers an interesting insight into the habits and character of sea eagles. Writing of a pair which were a 'great annoyance' to the neighbourhood of Baltasound on Unst, he notes '. . . so bold did they become at last, they would carry off poultry from the cottage doors when the men were at fishing, treating the women and children with the utmost contempt.' While this shows that the erne was probably bold enough to attack a young child, it leaves unanswered the question of whether an eagle would be capable of carrying even the tiniest of babies into the air. Many people will doubt that it ever happened, and there is little possibility of proving that it did.

But the genealogy is impeccable and can be verified by parish records as far back as the baptism of Mary Anderson's grandchildren. So who knows? Had Mary been killed by the eagle this book might never have been written.

Glossary of Shetland Wildlife Names

Birds

Aalin	Arctic Skua	*Stercorarius parasiticus*
Bonxie	Great Skua	*Stercorarius skua*
Calloo	Long-tailed Duck	*Clangula hyemalis*
Cockersüdies	Manx Shearwater	*Puffinus puffinus*
Erne	White-tailed Sea Eagle	*Haliaeetus albicilla*
Lintie	Twite	*Carduelis flavirostris*
Mally	Fulmar	*Fulmarus glacialis*
Stinkle or Stanechakker	Wheatear	*Oenanthe oenanthe*
Tystie	Black Guillemot	*Cepphus grylle*

Mammals

Caa'in whale	Pilot Whale	*Globicephala melaena*
Dratsie	Otter	*Lutra lutra*
Herring Hog	Minke Whale or Lesser Rorqual	*Balaenoptera acutorostrata*
Neesick	Common Porpoise	*Phocoena phocoena*
Whitret	Stoat	*Mustela erminea*

Fish

Banestickle	Three-spined Stickleback	*Gasterosteus aculeatus*
Hoe	Dogfish	*Scyliarhinus canicula*
Sillock	Saithe	*Pollachius virens*
Sulbregdi	Basking Shark	*Cetorhinus maximus*